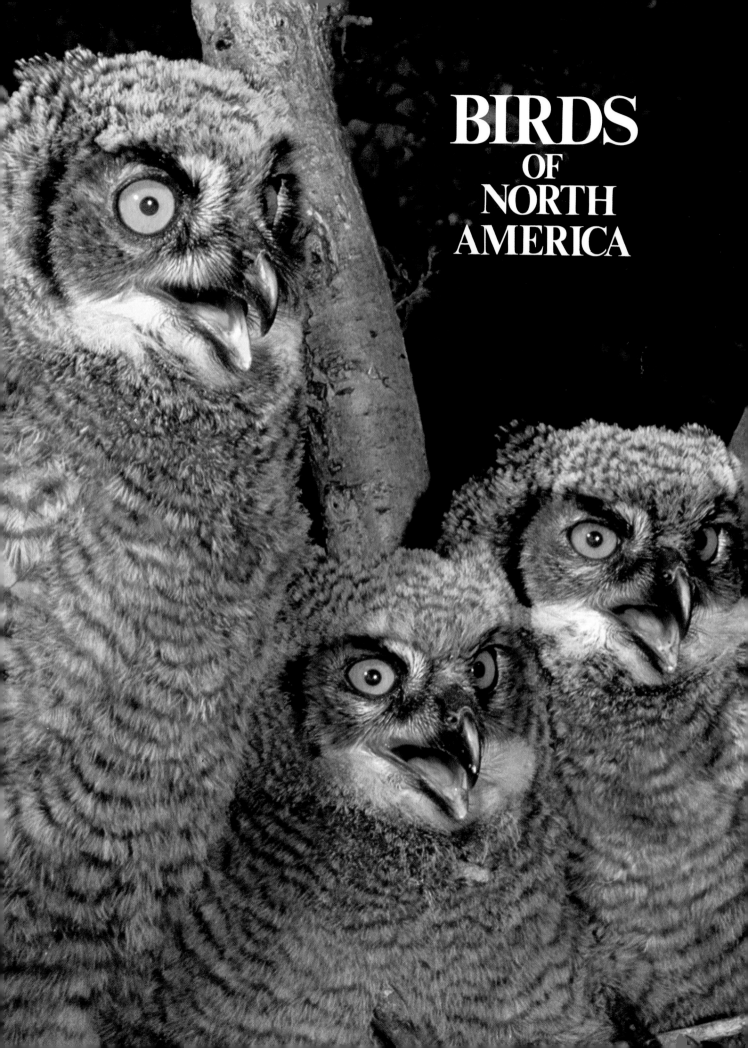

BIRDS
OF
NORTH
AMERICA

BIRDS
OF
NORTH AMERICA

Richard B. Lyttle

GALLERY BOOKS
An Imprint of W. H. Smith Publishers Inc.
112 Madison Avenue
New York City 10016

Published by Gallery Books
A Division of W. H. Smith Publishers Inc.
112 Madison Avenue
New York, New York 10016

Produced by
Bison Books Corp.
17 Sherwood Place
Greenwich, CT 06830
USA

Printed in Hong Kong

3 4 5 6 7 8 9 10

Library of Congress Catalog Card Number 82-81445

ISBN 0-8317-0877-8

Page 1: A threesome of Owls
Page 2-3: A Green Heron in the Florida Everglades.
Below: The Red-tailed Hawk is commonly seen perching high in trees or on a post. It lives wherever there are open spaces conducive to good hunting.

This book is for David Lavender

CONTENTS

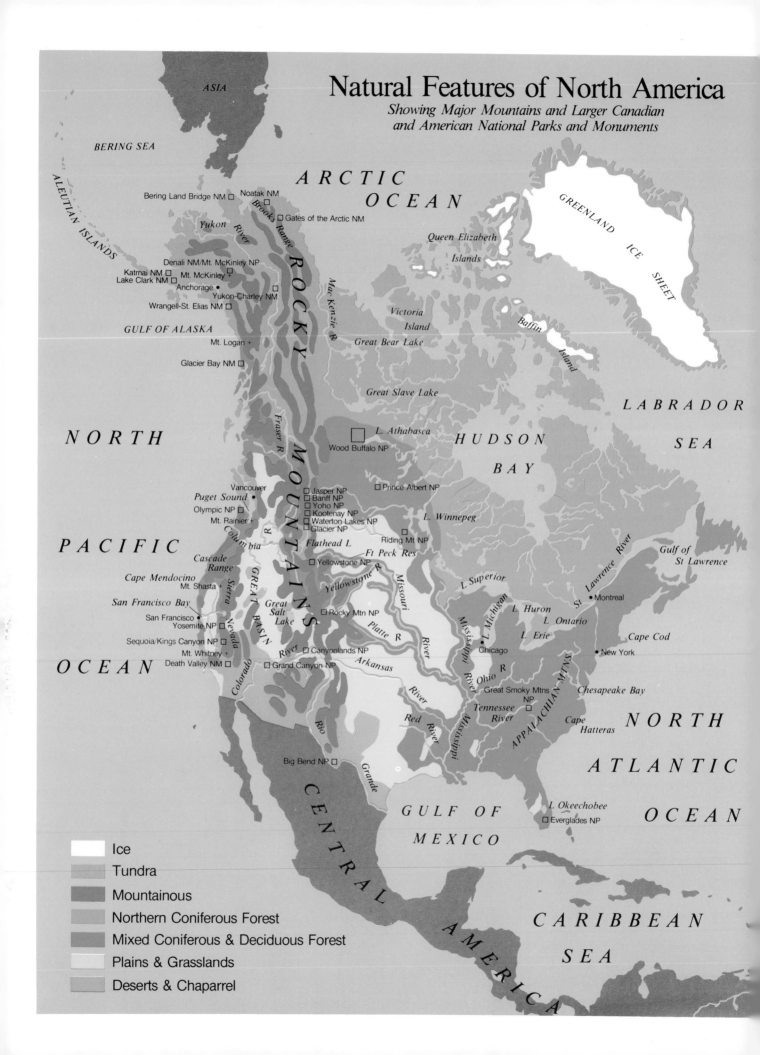

Natural Features of North America

Showing Major Mountains and Larger Canadian and American National Parks and Monuments

Legend:
- Ice
- Tundra
- Mountainous
- Northern Coniferous Forest
- Mixed Coniferous & Deciduous Forest
- Plains & Grasslands
- Deserts & Chaparrel

INTRODUCTION

North America is certainly not lacking in diversity of habitat. It ranges from wave-washed coasts to grass covered plains, from Arctic tundra and alpine peaks to arid deserts and humid woodlands. You might assume that the continent would support birdlife of great variety, but this is not exactly the case.

About 1,780 species of birds representing 97 bird families live and breed in North America. Many of these birds, however, are tropical species that do not venture out of Central America.

If we count only those birds seen regularly north of the Mexican border, the number drops to about 705 species, including 50 that breed elsewhere.

Compared with the world total of some 8,600 species, the variety of North American birdlife does seem some-what limited. Indeed, the continent is home for less than ten percent of all known birds. In terms of population totals, however, the numbers are more respectable. Most recent estimates of bird population which peaks in late summer, puts the North American census at 20 billion birds. This is a fifth of the world total in an area that represents 17 percent of the world's landmass.

For a bird lover, North America is thus a better than average place to watch, study, and enjoy birds. And it must be said that no single birdwatcher, not even the grayest veteran, has yet seen all birds of the continent.

Below: A Wilson's Phalarope (*Steganopus tricolor*) is the largest of the phalaropes and typical of its family in its reversal of sex roles.

Most birdwatchers, however, are less concerned about their life lists of identified species than they are about bird behavior. Here there is no limit to surprise, puzzlement, and fascination.

Bird migration can be studied in many regions of the world, but North America has four major migration flyways and great variety in seasonal shifting of individual bird populations. Some birds never leave their breeding grounds while others fly thousands of miles, unerringly following routes pioneered far back in geological time. How birds have inherited the routes and the traditional breeding spots that some return to generation after generation is just one of the mysteries of migration.

We do not yet fully understand the internal clock that triggers the migratory urge, and we do not know how birds navigate and home in on a destination.

Food finding presents other puzzles. The Clark's Nutcracker can locate summer caches of nuts months later even when they are hidden beneath several inches of snow. When a woodpecker taps a dead limb it may be using a form of sonar to locate a grub or worm by echo.

Bird intuition is uncanny. A Blue Jay will shriek its shrill warning at the first sight of a hungry house cat, but it will ignore the same animal when it is well fed.

A bird need certainly not be rare to attract the interest of a behaviorist. Flocks of common Redwing Blackbirds have a trait no one has yet explained. After roosting overnight in shrubs or trees, a flock with no apparent leadership will depart for its feeding grounds. Many birds fly separately in loose groups, but all arrive at the same field or meadow to feed. The place might be far from the previous day's feeding ground, but every member of the flock seems to get the message however it is passed.

Bird watchers of Europe will recognize several of the species described in this book. Many of the waterbirds particularly inhabit both the Old and New World. This is because they breed in the Arctic where landmasses of the two worlds almost join. Dispersion into both worlds has been the rule rather than the exception.

I have tried, however, to emphasize birds that are native to North America. I have also made an effort to avoid rare or casual visitors, birds that few might see in a lifetime of birdwatching. In the interest of the historical record, however, I have described some extinct or nearly extinct species. The California Condor, for instance, has all but vanished, but the cause of its failure is important to anyone who loves birds.

Division by regions is admittedly arbitrary, but the purpose of the book is to describe the prominent birds that are likely to be seen in various habitats. Serious birdwatchers who visit North America will obviously want to equip themselves with one or more of the excellent field guides that are available.

BIRDS OF NORTH AMERICA, a Guide to Field Identification (Golden Press, New York) by Chandler S Robbins, Bertel Bruun, and Herbert S Zim is a compact paperback with clear illustrations by Arthur Singer. For more detailed treatment Roger Tory Peterson, the dean of American birdwatchers, offers two books. *A FIELD GUIDE TO WESTERN BIRDS* and *A FIELD GUIDE TO EASTERN BIRDS* (both published by Houghton Mifflin Company, Boston) carry the author's own outstanding illustrations.

Those whose curiosity cannot be easily satisfied would do well to consult John K Terres' *THE AUDUBON SOCIETY ENCYCLOPEDIA OF NORTH AMERICAN BIRDS* (Alfred A Knopf, New York). This landmark work is illustrated with line drawings and excellent color plates by leading bird photographers.

Below: Young Starlings (*Sturnus vulgaris*) display the purple and green iridescence typical in spring.
Opposite: The Great Horned Owl (*Bubo virginianus*) is the largest and most familiar of the common owls.

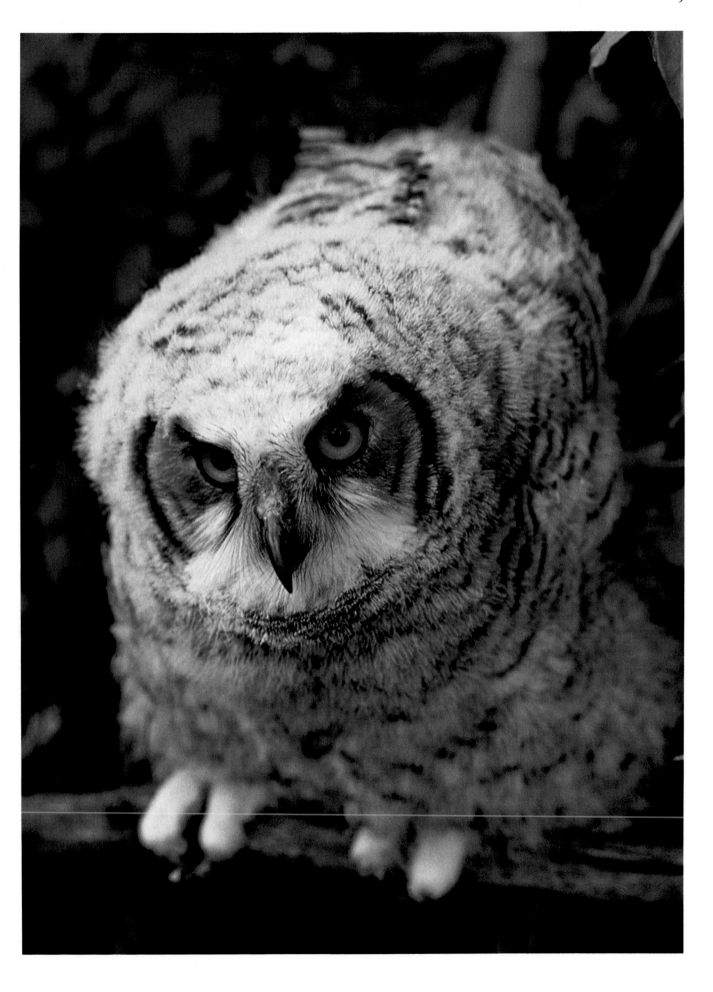

ARCTIC AND SUBARCTIC

For most months of the year the northern extremes of the continent—the tundra and the boreal forest—remain in the harsh grasp of winter. The monotony of the flat stretches of tundra might be relieved only by a snowy owl, and in its white plumage, even this bird is hard to see.

Although the spruce and fir of the boreal forest offer shelter, very few birds live year-round in this vast, subarctic region, and the few that do, such as the Pine Grosbeak, are hardy birds that have developed the ability to survive on a diet of pine nuts or other limited fare.

Bleak as these regions seem most of the year, both the tundra and the forest are transformed by summer. The tundra, with a surprising variety of plant life, attracts huge flocks of insect, bud, and seed eating birds. The sea, free of ice, attracts shore and water birds by the millions. And the forest becomes home for great populations of nesting birds.

All Arctic and subarctic migrants come to breed. In the short season they can raise but one brood, and many are forced to leave before they complete their post-nuptial molts. Several migrants such as the Golden Plover and the Arctic Tern fly great distances to take advantage of the Arctic's summer bounty.

The plover makes a 15,000 mile (24,155 kilometer) round trip annually between the Arctic coast and its wintering grounds in Argentina. The tern flies to the Antarctic and back each year to enjoy the summers of both hemispheres.

Other migrants, however, do not fly so far. Some arrive in the Arctic after wintering in the central or southern United States. Most of the shore birds winter along the coasts of Canada and the United States.

Although this section describes some common migrants such as loons and puffins, it concentrates more on the unusually hardy species that remain in or near the polar regions through all seasons.

Below: Arctic Terns (*Sterna paradisaea*) are distinguished from other terns by their red bill.
Opposite top: The Black Tern (*Chlidonias niger*) inhabits the more temperate bogs and marshes of Canada and the western United States.
Opposite bottom: Like the Black Tern, the Arctic Tern reacts to disturbances in a noisy fashion.
Overleaf: Special bacteria help the Rock Ptarmigan digest its winter diet of buds and twigs.

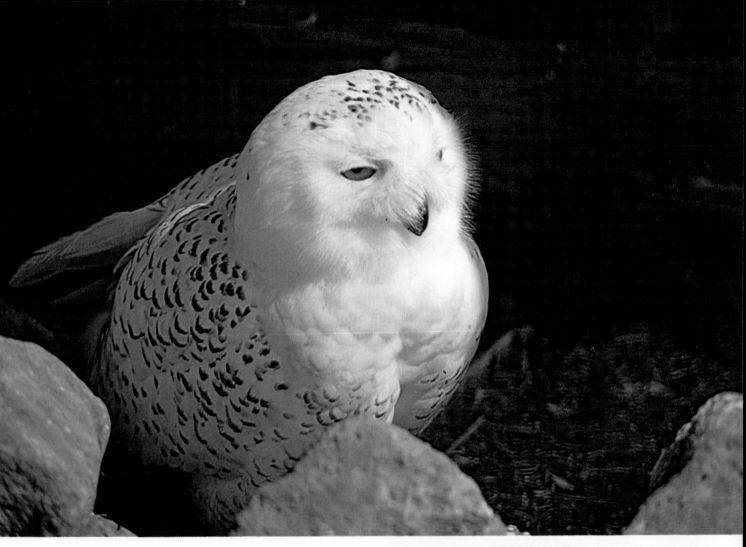

Snowy Owl

Strongest and heaviest of North American owls, the Snowy Owl *(Nyctea scaniaca)* inhabits the Arctic regions of both the Old and New World. Periodically, however, when food is scarce, it moves south into southern Canada and the northern states of the US.

The southern invasion is triggered by a drop in the population of lemmings, the Snowy Owl's favorite prey. The lemming supply also influences the birds' nesting and egg laying. When the lemmings are very scarce, Snowy Owls often will not nest at all. And when they do nest, clutches will vary from as little as three to as many as 13 eggs. The more lemmings, the bigger the clutch.

Actually, a Snowy will eat almost anything that it can catch. It will wade into the water to snatch fish with its talons. It preys on ptarmigans, grebes, small gulls, ducks, young geese, and crows. When hunger drives it south, it will hunt rabbits, ground squirrels, rats, weasels, moles, and shrews. It has even been known to eat carrion.

The bird is 20 to 27 inches (50.8 to 68.5 cm) long and has a wingspread of 55 to 66 inches (139.7 to 167.6 cm). Aver-

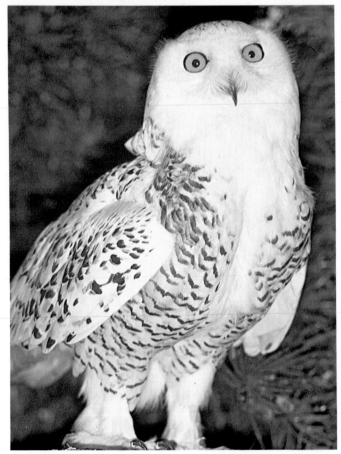

Above and right: The Snowy Owl lays its eggs in a hollow lined with moss or grass in the dry ground of the tundra.
Opposite: The Evening Grosbeak was originally sighted at twilight and thus designated as a 'night singer.' The name has remained, though wrong.

age weight for males is 3.63 pounds (1.650 grams) and for females 4.31 pounds (1.960 grams).

No other white bird is so heavily built. It has a large round head with no ear tufts, yellow eyes, and often brown bars on wings and body. Barring is heaviest on young birds. Females also may show more barring than males.

Because its normal habitat is the treeless tundra, it is a ground percher and retains a preference for low perches such as rocks or fence posts even when it moves into a forested area. A daytime hunter, the perching bird keeps a sharp eye out for prey and for enemies. It will rarely let man approach closer than 200 feet (61 m).

Although the upstrokes of its flight seem jerky, its downstrokes are strong. Its top flying speed has been clocked at 50 miles (80.5 km) an hour.

The owl has a variety of calls, including a shrill whistle, a growl, and a croak as well as a deep hoot. The hoot, sounded from a ground perch, is a territorial song and can be heard any time of day. Hooting has been known to carry two miles.

Although nesting can begin in late May, it usually does not start until the second week in June. The female begins incubating her eggs as soon as the first one is laid. Thus, the hatch, which takes 32 or 33 days of incubation, is spread over several days and the chicks show considerable size differences.

When about 16 days old, the chicks leave the nest, little more than a hollow in the earth, and perch on the nearby tundra. The male continues to feed them until all chicks have left the nest. Then the female helps feed the young. First flights occur 43 to 57 days after hatching.

Adult birds use the crippled bird act to decoy predators away from the nest and chicks. Male Snowys have been known to defend the nest against wolves and foxes.

Pine Grosbeak

One of the northernmost representatives of the Finch or *Fringillidae* family, the red to pink Pine Grosbeak is a relatively large bird and has a heavy, triangular bill that enables it to feed year-round in the conifer forests of the subarctic.

Although it will eat insects, its diet is made up mainly of seeds of pine, spruce, and fir trees which it extracts from cones with its strong bill. In years of short seed supply or when population of the seed eaters is abnormally high, flocks of grosbeaks invade southern latitudes where their diet becomes more varied.

In addition to nuts of both hardwoods and conifers, Pine Grosbeaks will also eat berries and seeds of many different plants. They are particularly fond of sunflower seeds which are often used to attract them to feeding stations.

The Pine Grosbeak *(Pinicola enucleator)* is one of 436 members of the Finch family, 83 of which are found in North America. Others in the family include crossbills, cardinals, juncos, sparrows, buntings, goldfinches, rosy finches, and finches. The Evening Grosbeak *(Hesperiphona vespertina)*, a yellow and black bird, is also found in the

northern forests, but it does not range as far north and often flies farther south than the Pine Grosbeak. Both birds are also found in northern forests of Eurasia.

The Black-headed Grosbeak *(Pheucticus melanocephalus)* and the Blue Grosbeak *(Guiraca caerulea)* inhabit the forest-covered mountains well south of the Pine Grosbeak's range.

The male bird, 8 to 10 inches (20.3 to 25.4 cm) long, has a red to rosy body specked with gray. Its slightly forked tail, back, and wings are gray to black. The wings are barred with white. The eyes and beak are black. Female and young birds have gray to brown bodies.

Its lack of contact with man apparently makes the Pine Grosbeak bold. It can sometimes be picked up in the hands. It is also highly social, gathering in flocks of 100 or more when it makes its winter visits to the northern states. In early spring, however, pairing begins and flocks break up.

The nesting season usually begins in May when a bulky structure of twigs, roots, and grasses is built in the fork of a tree from 6 to 30 feet (1.8 to 9.1 m) above the ground. Usually four blue-green to gray-green eggs, patterned with brown or gray, are laid. The female, fed by the male, incubates the eggs for two weeks. Young birds leave the nest when they are three weeks old.

Snow Bunting

Nesting farther north than any other land bird, the Snow Bunting *(Plectrophenax nivalis)* is a winter visitor to the heavily populated regions of Canada and the United States. Here it is seen in large flocks, often during snow storms.

Although its white winter plumage is patterned with black, tawny brown, and cinnamon, it appears almost entirely white when flying. This has earned it the alternate names of Snowbird and Snowflake.

The Snow Bunting can survive at −58°F (−50°C), but many sometimes die if late Arctic snow covers the food supply.

Another member of the finch family, the Snow Bunting is a ground feeder with a strong bill. And like most other finches it is a migrant.

The bird, from 6 to 7¼ inches (15.2 to 18.4 cm) long, is often seen feeding around haystacks, barnyards, or trash heaps. It can also be found among dunes, on open beaches, and at the edge of salt marshes. It will roost on the ground in the shelter of low vegetation, and it often can be seen bathing in snow. In extreme cold, it will burrow into the snow to keep warm.

Although it has been seen as far south as Alabama, Georgia, and even Florida, it prefers the cooler climates found from the central states north. Some birds even winter in central and southern Alaska.

The birds start north in late March. Large flocks of whistling and trilling birds mark the beginning of migration. The bunting's breeding range is circumpolar. In North America it extends from Greenland to Alaska and includes many of the Arctic islands.

Opposite: The Snow Bunting can often be seen in large, mixed flocks hunting for seeds in grasslands or in fields.
Below: The Common Loon tends to make its wild, tremolo call during the breeding period but remains quiet during migration.

Breeding plumage shows sharp contrast between black tail and back and white cap and underparts. Females are paler than males.

Egg laying begins in May usually with four to seven eggs in a ground nest hidden under moss or in crevices between rocks. The female incubates the eggs for the 10 to 15 days it takes them to hatch. Young may leave the nest after just ten days and begin flying just 13 days after hatching. Unlike most other Arctic migrants, Snow Buntings sometimes raise two broods in one season.

The slightly larger all white McKay's Bunting *(Plectrophenax hyperboreus)* is a close relative of the Snow Bunting, but it has a more limited range. It nests on the islands of the Bering Sea, and while some birds move south to winter along the Alaskan coast, many birds summer on their breeding islands.

Other buntings in North America, the Lark, Indigo, Lazuli, Painted, and Varied Buntings, all more colorful than the Snow and McKay's Buntings, do not range nearly as far north to raise their young.

Arctic Loon

The Arctic Loon, also known as the Arctic Diver, Black-throated Diver, or Pacific Loon, is one of four members of the Loon or *Gavidae* family.

All four breed in the Arctic and winter in the lower latitudes of the Northern Hemisphere. The Arctic Loon *(Gavia arctica)* winters along the Pacific Coast as far south as the Gulf of California. Rarely is it seen on the Atlantic Coast.

With strong migratory drives, all loons go through a seasonal change in plumage. The breeding plumage, usually with dark back and white belly, also includes delicate white and black patterns on the neck, sides and back. Winter plumage is generally dull gray above and white below with white often on the front part of the neck.

The Arctic Loon, 23 to 29 inches (58.4 to 73.7 cm) long, has a summer pattern of white, vertical stripes on the sides of its black neck. The crown and back of the neck are gray. The large Common Loon *(Gavia immer)* has a collar of white and black horizontal stripes contrasting with a black head and neck.

In winter, however, both birds look similar, except that the Arctic Loon is smaller. The Red-throated Loon *(Gavia stellata),* the most widely distributed of the family, has a sharply angled lower mandible that gives its bill an upswept appearance lacking in the other loons. The Yellow-billed Loon *(Gavia adamsii),* the largest of the loons, can be distinguished from the others by its yellow bill. The Yellow-billed Loon also winters on the Pacific Coast and is rarely seen in the east.

All loons are great divers, sometimes chasing small fish to depths of 240 feet (73.2 m). They can stay below at least a full minute and surface a surprising distance from the spot where they began their dive. Loons' legs are positioned well back on the body for efficient propulsion in the water. The legs, however, are poorly adopted for walking. Most loons cannot take off from the land.

Above and below: The Tufted Puffin dwells on the sea cliffs and feeds in the cold waters. These birds nest in large colonies with thousands of other puffins.
Opposite: The last surviving colony of the Great Auk was killed off in Iceland in 1844. The skin, bones and eggs of these birds are now precious treasures.

The birds have special muscle cells that allow them to store extra oxygen for long dives, and many tissues and organs are designed to function on low oxygen supply.

Like other loons, the Arctic Loon is very vocal, with the high-pitched call of *aaaa-ha-weee* and the eerie 'laughter' that prompted the expression 'crazy as a loon'. Arctic Loons also utter duck-like *quacks* and low-pitched *chucks*.

A solitary nester, the Arctic Loon prefers the shores of large freshwater lakes for its breeding site. Birds will, however, nest in the open tundra, in forested areas, or even in the mountains a good distance from water. The nests vary from scrapes in soft ground to mounds built up of vegetable matter. One or two green to brown eggs are laid in June or July.

Incubation by both birds takes about a month. Chicks can swim soon after hatching, but they do not fly until they are about 60 days old. Young chicks often climb on a parent bird's back to rest and avoid aquatic predators.

While some birds move to nearby open water to winter close to their nesting grounds, most fly south, well below the Arctic latitudes.

Tufted Puffin

Bizarre in appearance, the Tufted Puffin and its family hold an odd niche in bird evolution.

Along with the razorbill, dovekie, murre, murrelet, auk, auklet, and guillemot, the puffin belongs to the Auk or

Alcidae family, the members of which have been described as the penguins of the North. The flightless Great Auk *(Pinguinus impennis)*, now extinct, was in fact the first bird to be called a penguin. Later the same name was applied to the flightless birds of the Antarctic.

Although not related to penguins, members of the Auk family have many similar traits. They are salt water birds with short, stout beaks, chunky bodies well insulated with plumage, and short wings that they use to 'fly' underwater. They are mostly black and white, live largely on fish, and become landlubbers only during the breeding season when, like penguins, they gather in large colonies.

Although there is some southern movement to escape the severity of northern winters, most *Alcids* simply disperse into the seas after the breeding season.

The Tufted Puffin *(Lunda cirrhata)*, the largest of the three North American puffins, is also the most widely distributed. Its breeding range extends from northwest Alaska and the Aleutian Islands south on both sides of the Pacific as far as Japan in the East and Southern California in the West. Sightings on the Atlantic Coast are listed as accidental.

The Common Puffin *(Fratercula arctica)* and the Horned Puffin *(Fratercula corniculata)* have white bellies, but except for its large, orange bill, orange legs, white face mask and ear tufts of pale straw, the Tufted Puffin is a black bird. Young birds show some browns and grays, but adults of both sexes have jet black plumage.

The bird, 14½ to 15½ inches (36.8 to 39.3 cm) long, loses its tufts after the breeding season, but it can still be distinguished from the other puffins which show white sides and bellies.

Puffins, skillful divers and underwater swimmers, catch smelt, sardines, and herrings, some up to 10 inches (25.4 cm) long. They are not as adept in the air where they must keep their short wings beating rapidly to stay aloft.

The breeding season runs from April to July in the southern end of the range and from June to July in the northern limits. Each pair in the colony scoops out a hollow in the bare earth where just one, pale blue egg, spotted with brown or lavender, is laid. Both birds share incubation duties, but the time of incubation and the age of young when they fly is not yet known. Some birds in the southern areas, however, may brood twice each season.

The Tufted Puffin is also called Old Man of the Sea and Sea Parrot, both apt names.

White-tailed Ptarmigan

Of the three ptarmigans found in North America, the White-tailed Ptarmigan *(Lagopus leucurus)* ranges farthest into high altitudes and thus inhabits both the Arctic and alpine regions well to the south.

The White-tail is seen on the snowy slopes of the Cascades and Rocky Mountains, and recent transplants of the bird in the Sierra Nevada appear to have been successful.

Right: A White-tailed Ptarmigan, smallest of ptarmigans.

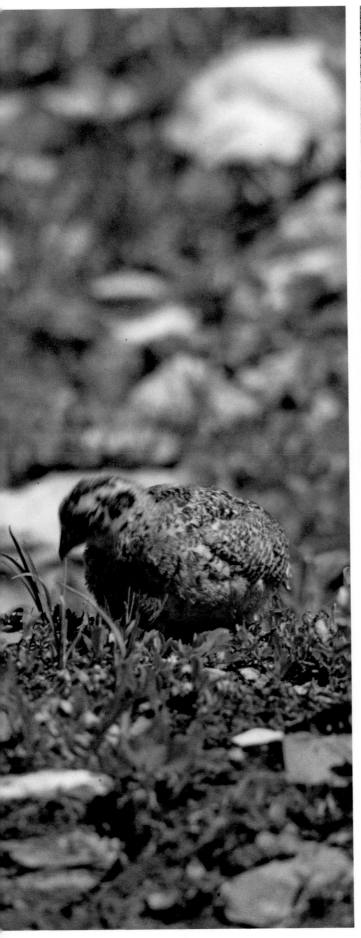

Left and above: In the winter the feathers of the Rock Ptarmigan turn white, except for part of the male tail and lores which remain black. White feathers are composed of empty cells of air which insulate.

The Rock Ptarmigan *(Lagopus mutus)* and Willow Ptarmigan *(Lagopus lagopus)* are rarely seen south of the Arctic Circle. The White-tail is also unique to the New World while the two other ptarmigans are circumpolar.

The smallest of the three, the White-tailed Ptarmigan is 12 to 13 inches (30.5 to 33 cm) long. All white in winter, the body turns brown in summer. The tail, wings, and belly, however, remain white. The white tail sets the bird apart from the other two ptarmigans who have brown tails. And the white wings prevent confusing the White-tailed Ptarmigan with the nine other North American members of the Grouse or *Tetraodinae* family.

Feeding and roosting habits are similar for all ptarmigans. They are swift fliers and often rise from cover with an explosive burst that startles predators. They will roost beneath the snow and sometimes avoid leaving tell-tale tracks to their burrows by diving directly into a snow bank. It is not unusual for a dozen or more birds to be buried in the same bank.

Ptarmigans have tufts of feathers over their nostrils to allow them to breathe under the snow. They also grow a winter matting of feathers on their feet to keep them from

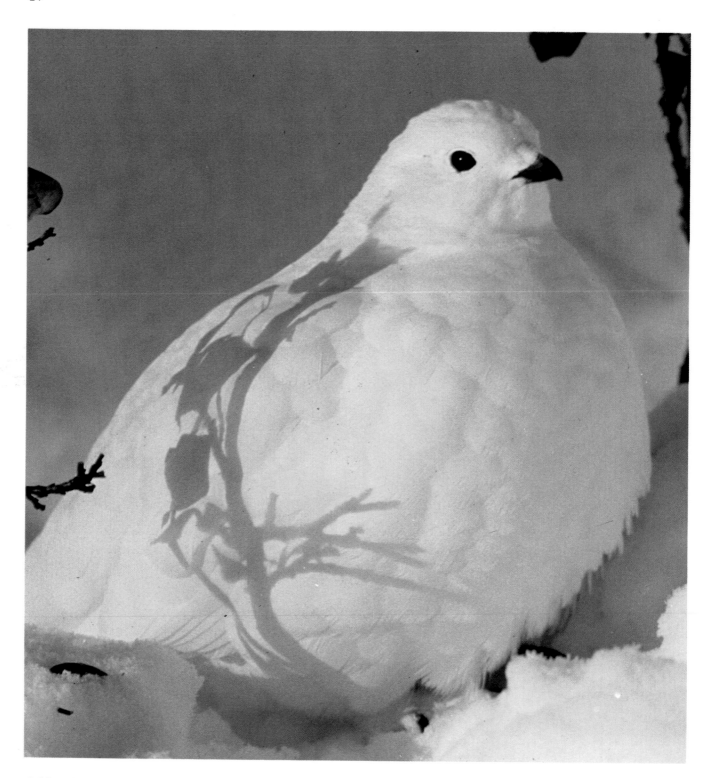

sinking through the surface of the snow when browsing for food. The birds subsist largely on tender shoots of the Arctic willow, the dominant plant of the tundra.

The nest of the White-tailed Ptarmigan is a shallow depression in short grass usually on a steep slope where scattered rocks offer shelter. With good protective coloring, the hen will remain on her eggs almost until stepped upon.

Clutches range from four to 16 eggs which are believed to hatch in about 24 days. The chicks leave the nest under the hen's protection soon after hatching. In about ten days, they can fly several feet.

Because of its small size, the White-tailed Ptarmigan is sometimes confused with quail. In fact, common names in some regions are White Quail, Snow Quail, and Mountain Quail. But the quail, although a ground feeder, is a member of the Pheasant, not the Grouse family.

Long-tailed Jaeger

There are still many mysteries about birds, and the winter range of the Long-tailed Jaeger *(Stercorarius long-icaudus)* is one of them.

Opposite: A White-tailed Ptarmigan in winter plumage.
Above: A Rock Ptarmigan with chicks.
Right: The common Willow Ptarmigan of the Arctic.

In summer the birds nest in the tundra all around the Arctic, but in winter they take to sea, apparently to wander and scavenge over a wide area, perhaps down to 50° south latitude in both the Atlantic and the Pacific, but the patterns of movement vary. When lemmings, the Long-tailed Jaeger's chief summer food, are scarce, which happens every three or four years, the birds do not appear on their usual nesting grounds. They either breed or simply wait out the summer elsewhere.

As members of the Skua or *Stercoraridae* Family, jaegers are birds of prey. In the northern regions they fill the

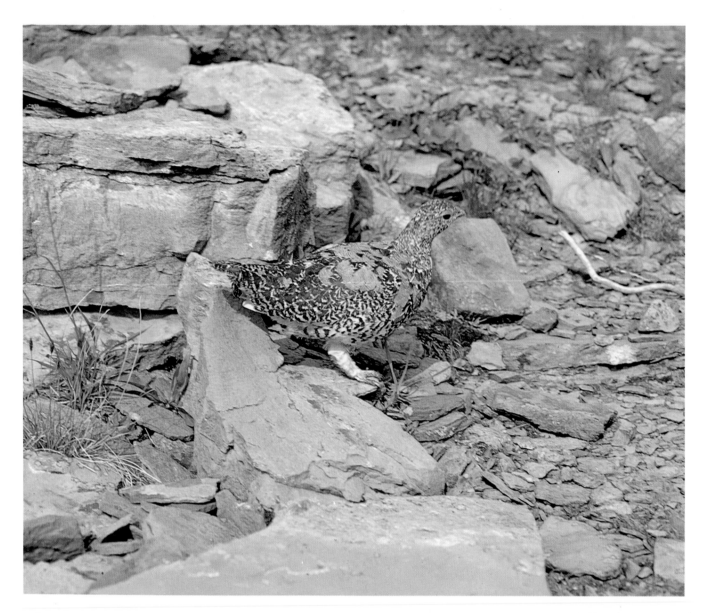

roll of hawks and vultures. They look like gulls but are generally more agile in flight. Skuas also have a fleshy ridge or cere around the nostrils that gulls lack. The three North American jaegers are further distinguished by having elongated central tail feathers. The Long-tailed Jaeger's tail feathers, up to 8 inches (20.3 cm) long, set it apart from the Parasite Jaeger *(Stercorarius parasiticus)* and the Pomarine Jaeger *(Stercorarius pomarinus)*.

The Long-tailed Jaeger is 20 to 23 inches (50.8 to 58.4 cm) long and has a wingspread of about 30 inches (76.2 cm). It has a white body with black to gray brown tail and wings and a black cap that extends down the face just a little below eye level.

Like other jaegers, it will attack gulls and terns, forcing them to disgorge recently caught fish, but the Long-tailed Jaeger is an accomplished hunter in its own right. It will hover above the tundra for several seconds before swooping down for a rodent or insect. It catches fish in the same manner, and it also attacks nests of other birds to take eggs and chicks. Late in the breeding season, it feeds on berries, particularly crowberries.

Birds arrive in the Arctic in May and nesting usually begins within a month. The nest is a depression in high ground that is lined with grass or other bits of vegetable matter loosely scraped together. Usually two brown eggs with dark spots are laid. Incubation by both birds takes about 23 days.

Jaegers defend their nest with vigor, attacking Arctic foxes and even humams who venture too close. Birds have flown directly into a man's face to protect the nest. Jaegers also use the wounded bird decoy to lure an intruder away from the nest.

Young birds can fly about 21 days after hatching. Families, however, stay together and apparently are still together when they leave the Arctic at the end of the season for parts unknown.

Above: A Rock Ptarmigan cackles noisily when alarmed.
Opposite top: The size of a chicken, the Ruffed Grouse *(Bonasa umbellus)* inhabits deciduous woodlands.
Opposite bottom: The Blue Grouse *(Dendragapus obscurus)* dwells in coastal forests, mainly west of the Rockies.

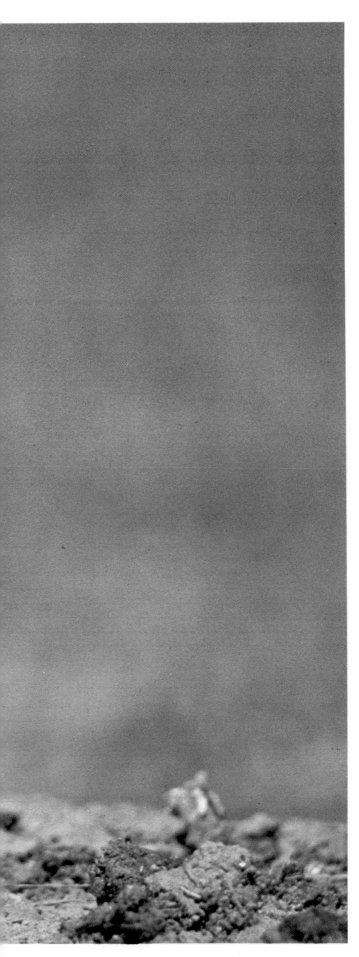

DESERTS

Compared with the hot sands of the Sahara, the North America desert is the promised land. Animal and plant life, though not teeming, occurs in some regions with surprising variety.

Actually there are many different kinds of desert or near desert found in the southwest and the basin country between the coastal ranges and the Rocky Mountains. All are arid due to the weather pattern over the western side of the continent.

As Pacific storms move inland across the Sierra Nevada, Cascades, and other coastal mountains, they are forced up into cooling air which wrings out most of the moisture in rain and snow. East of the mountains there is thus very little precipitation left for a thirsty land.

Despite the variety of American deserts, they fall generally into two groups—the cold desert of the basin states, and the hot deserts of the southwest. The hot deserts support vast stands of cacti while the cold deserts are thinly blanketed with sagebrush. The bird life of the hot deserts is far more diverse than the bird life of the cold deserts.

The imbalance is due largely to the difference in growth of the two regions. Sagebrush, related to the wormwood of the Old World, nourishes a very small population of insects. Insect-eating birds, therefore, are rare in the cold deserts.

Because it feeds directly on sage leaves, buds, and flowers, the Sage Grouse is one of the few birds that has found a happy niche in the cold deserts.

The hot deserts of southeastern California, Arizona, New Mexico, and western Texas abound with cacti and other hardy plants that can survive long periods of drought. And when rare rains do fall, the plants burst with bloom and produce bumper crops of seeds. Seeds and insects support a community of life with food chains often as complex as those found in more verdant regions.

Birds like the Gambel's Quail feed almost exclusively on seeds. Others like the Cactus Wren eat both seeds and insects, while the Gila Woodpecker and Elf Owl exist almost entirely on insects. The Roadrunner preys upon small reptiles, mammals, and insects, while the ubiquitous Turkey Vulture, which includes the arid lands in its wide range, feeds on the desert's dead.

There is some migratory movement in the deserts, but it is just as likely to be oriented up and down nearby mountains as it is in a north and south axis. As spring blooms move up a mountain slope so do the birds, and down they come again when snows descend.

But rarely are the hot deserts silent.

Left: The Burrowing Owl (*Athene cunicularia*) is a small owl which inhabits the open country areas such as deserts, sand dunes, fallow fields and prairies.

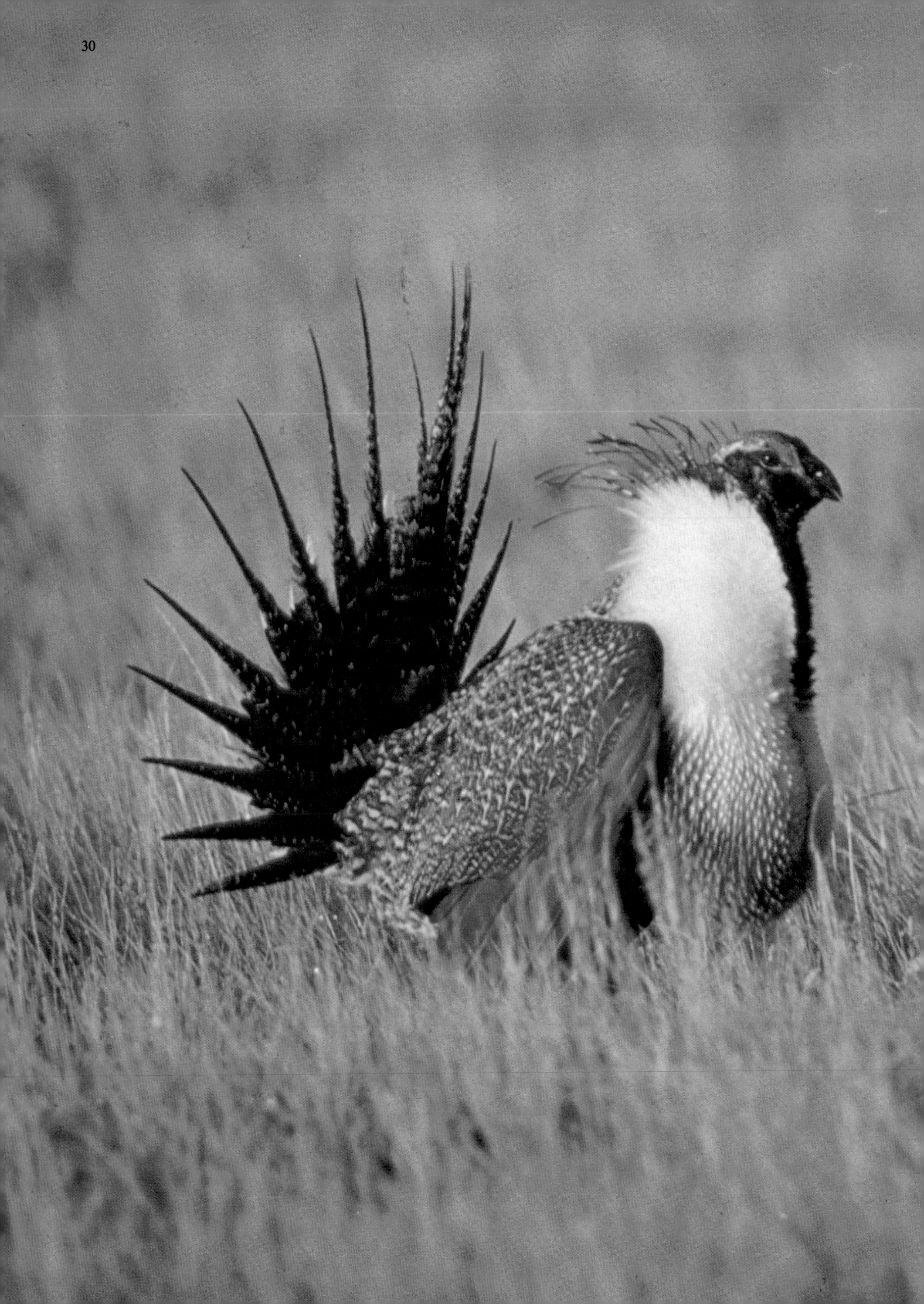

The Sage Grouse nests and hides in the sagebrush and eats the leaves and buds.

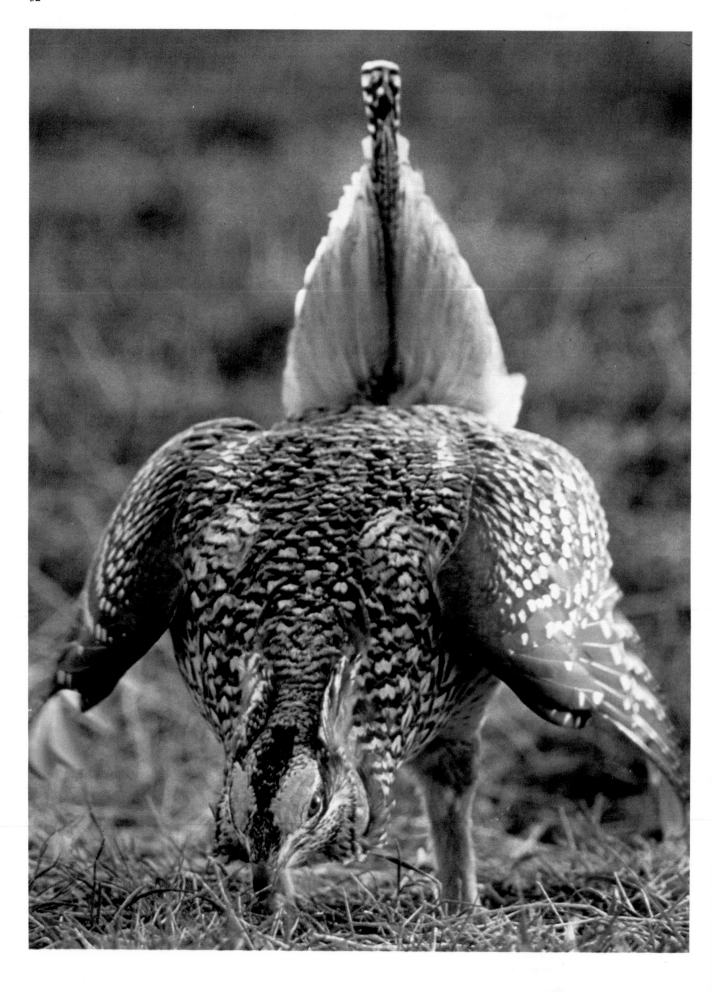

Sage Grouse

The largest representative of its family in North America, the Sage Grouse *(Centrocercus urophasianus)* has a gray-brown plumage which blends perfectly with the sagebrush of its arid habitat.

With a maximum body length of 30 inches (76.2 cm) and a weight of six pounds (2.72 kg), the male Sage Grouse is often twice the size of the female. And the male is impressive, particularly during its unusual courtship dance.

Both male and female have black bellies and stiff, pointed tail feathers, but the male has a white breast and black throat marked by a contrasting bar of white. In flight, the female dips from side to side as it rises, while the male rises steadily without dipping.

Sage Grouse lack the digestive system necessary for eating hard grains and seeds. Thus their diet is limited to soft shoots of plants, particularly sagebrush. They also eat insects such as ants and grasshoppers. When they are finished browsing, Grouse often roost in a circle on the ground.

A popular game bird, some 250,000 are shot each year. The main threat to its survival, however, is loss of habitat

Opposite: Sharp-tailed Grouse (*Pedioecetes phasianellus*), like many grouse, perform intricate courtship displays and return to the same place annually to breed.
Below: The California Quail feeds on the ground but withdraws to the trees for roosting and protection.

due to encroachment of livestock grazing into the intermountain plains. Still, the Sage Grouse is luckier than the closely related Prairie Chicken whose habitat has largely been lost to the plow.

The Sage Grouse is a classic example of an arena bird, and the arena for the males' courtship dances may be 200 yards (182.8 m) wide and half a mile (805 m) long.

Courtship begins when some 400 male birds gather on the arena. The birds stay 25 to 40 feet (7.6 to 12.2 m) apart, but the strongest cocks have favored positions near the center of the arena.

The cocks extend their tail feathers to form an upright fan and inflate two yellow air sacks in their breast. The wings are held against their sides so that the primaries frame the display of air sacks. As the cocks strut, the females gather.

The females try to select the most magnificent males for their mates. Copulation occurs on the arena. The result of the unusual courtship is that about ten percent of the males service about 75 percent of the females. One cock was observed copulating with 21 hens in one morning.

No pair bonds are formed. Female Sage Grouse hollow out a shallow depression beneath a small bush and lay 7 to 14 eggs. Egg laying begins as early as mid-March in some regions. Incubation takes 25 to 27 days, and young Grouse can fly seven to 14 days after they hatch.

Sage Grouse do not migrate, but remain year-round in arid regions of Washington, Oregon, Idaho, Montana, North Dakota, Alberta and Saskatchewan south into central California, Nevada, Utah and Colorado.

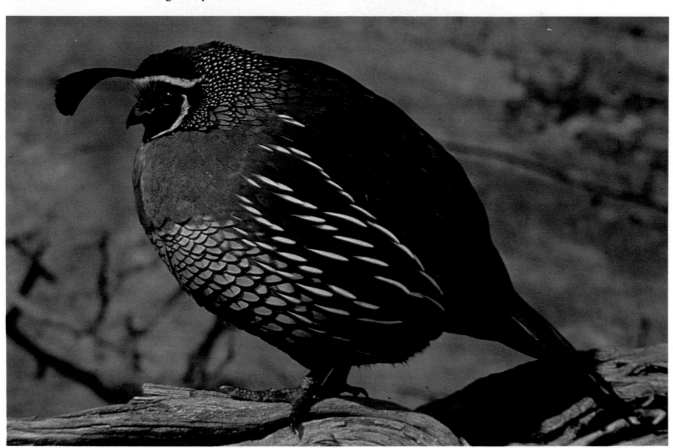

Gambel's Quail

Near springs and streams the identifying call of the Gambel's Quail *(Lophortyx gambelii)* may be the song that most typifies life in the hot deserts. The four-note *chi-CA-go-go* may sound unvaried to human ears, but each bird has its own slight but identifying inflection.

The call is invariably heard when a bird becomes separated from its covey. The low chuckles and grunts of contentment made by birds when they are together does not carry nearly as far as the identifying call. The Gambel's, some 9½ to 11 inches (23.6 to 27.9 cm) long, is the same size as the California Quail *(Lophortyx californicus)* which it resembles closely.

Although both birds have black plumes which curve forward to end in a teardrop above the forehead, the Gambel's has a more russet crest and sides than the California Quail. The male Gambel's also has a black patch in the middle of its white belly while the California Quail has a scaled pattern on its breast and belly.

Confusion of species in any case is not likely because the California Quail generally avoids the arid territory where the Gambel's flourishes.

Like most Quail of the New World, the Gambel's is a social species during the non-breeding season. Coveys, sometimes made up of as many as 50 birds, will contain several families. The large groups help the birds avoid surprise attacks by predators. The moment one bird is alarmed into flight, all birds fly for cover. With a top flying speed of 41 miles (66 km) an hour, the bird is a difficult target both for predator and hunter.

Above: At the end of the breeding season flocks of California Quail can be seen in some city parks and yards.
Right: The Gambel's Quail loses large numbers of its nests to predators in the desert.

As early as March, the coveys break up as birds pair to defend territory and build nests which are often simply grass and feather-lined scrapes at the base of a shrub. Sometimes the Quail will use the abandoned nest of other birds such as the Roadrunner or Cactus Wren.

The female alone incubates a clutch of 10 to 12 eggs, but the male can usually be found guarding nearby. After the chicks hatch in 21 to 23 days, they are ready at once to leave the nest and be herded by the adult birds in search of grass seeds and cactus fruit. Usually the brood is led by the male and followed by the female.

At time of danger, the chicks seem to know instinctively that their best defense is their protective coloring. When they crouch motionless on dead leaves they are all but impossible to see.

In the fall, when the chicks have reached maturity, the families band together into coveys once again. Favorite spots for coveys are low valleys where the mesquite or other cover is dense. The birds also like to feed beneath the willows along the banks of streams. At night, the low branches of willows provide convenient roosts.

Gambel's Quail are early feeders, dropping from their roosts at first light to forage for seeds, berries, and fruits for several hours. By early afternoon, however, when temperatures reach their peak, the birds are resting in the shade.

The species is found in arid regions of Nevada, Utah, Colorado, New Mexico, Texas, Arizona, Baja California and Sonora. In Arizona, it has the dubious honor of being the most hunted game bird.

Cactus Wren

Like the other nine representatives of the Wren or *Troglodytidae* family in North America, the Cactus Wren is a great nest builder. Actually, the male of this species, who does all the work, is an over-builder, making many more nests than are needed each season.

Nest building habits, more than preference for arid regions, are believed to limit the range of the Cactus Wren *(Campylorhynchus brunneicapillus)*. The male selects the low branches of thorny shrubs and trees typical of arid climates for the nest site. The nest itself is bulb-shaped with a tunnel side entrance, and the tunnel opening is located to take maximum advantage of the protecting growth.

A mated pair will use its brood nest and other spares built in the territory as year-round roosts. Old brood nests are not abandoned but maintained instead as part of the roost nest inventory.

The state bird of Arizona, the Cactus Wren is 7 to 8 ¾ inches (17.7 to 22.2 cm) long, making it the largest Wren in North America. Mostly rusty brown, the bird has a con-

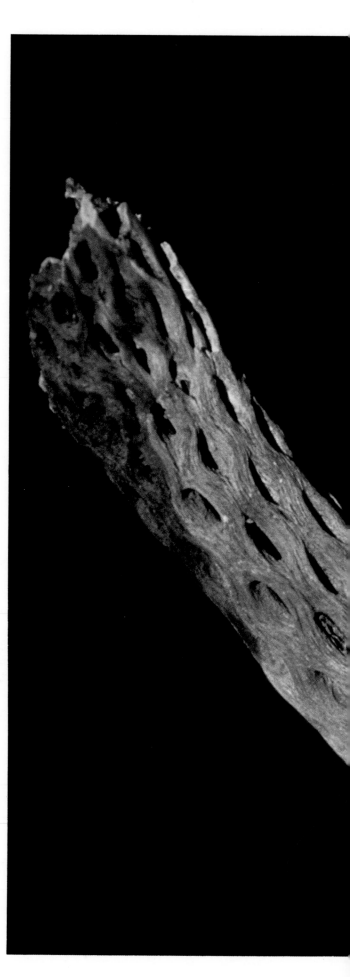

Right: Cactus Wrens maintain their nests and will retreat to them for protection from the rain.
Overleaf: The Gila Woodpecker is one of 20 species of woodpeckers which inhabit North America. It finds food on the ground or by chiseling tree bark.

spicuous white stripe over each eye. and in flight it shows bars of white on its outer tail feathers.

Although it will eat seeds. berries. and cactus fruit. its diet is made up mostly of beetles. ants. wasps. grasshoppers. bugs. and spiders. It has also been known to eat lizards and tree frogs.

Typically. a ground foraging Cactus Wren slips its bill under a moveable object such as a dead leaf to lift it up and look for any insect that might be hiding there.

Nesting. which can begin as early as March. sometimes continues into August with one pair raising as many as three broods.

Incubation of the four or five white to pale pink eggs takes 16 days. and the young usually leave the nest 19 to 23 days after hatching.

Cactus Wrens are found in arid regions of Southern California. Nevada. Arizona. Utah. New Mexico. Texas and northwestern Mexico. Its deep-throated *chuh-chuh-chuh-chuh* may be the first indication and often the only hint of its presence. For. like other Wrens. this species is a shy bird.

The Winter Wren *(Troglodytes troglodytes)*, about half the size of the Cactus Wren and widely distributed in high latitudes of North America. is the only member of the family found in the Old World where it is known simply as the Wren.

All Wrens. it is believed. evolved in the New World. but the Winter Wren extended its range. probably by way of Alaska. into Eurasia and Africa.

Gila Woodpecker

Because of their undulating flight and ability to cling to the vertical trunks of trees. members of the Woodpecker Family are easily recognized. And in the deserts of Nevada. Arizona. and New Mexico. the most common species is the Gila Woodpecker *(Melanerpes uropygialis).*

Both male and female have fawn colored bodies 8 to 10 inches (20.3 to 25.4 cm) long with tails and wings barred black and white. This gives them a zebra-backed appearance when perched. In flight. the birds show a white patch near the tip of each wing. Male birds have a crown patch of red which the females lack.

Most abundant on Arizona's arid mesas. Gila Woodpeckers prefer to hollow out their nests in the giant saguaro cactus. But they will also nest in cottonwoods. sycamores. and willows. The entrance hole of the nest. about two inches (5.1 cm) in diameter. leads to an excavated bowl nine to 20 inches (22.9 to 50.8 cm) deep.

A mated pair will use the same nest more than one season. but usually they must build a new one because the nest of the previous season will have been taken over by an Owl. Cactus Wren. or Flycatcher.

Like other Woodpeckers. the Gila Woodpecker flies with a series of rapid flaps broken by a folded-wing glide. This gives the characteristic undulating flight. The bird. noisy when perched. also utters sharp cries in flight which sound something like *pit* or *huit.*

The bird's sharp claws and stiff tail feathers allow it to 'perch' vertically on the trunks of trees where it finds the insects which make up the bulk of its diet. Grubs. ants. beetles and grasshoppers are its favorite fare. but it will also eat berries. fruit and occasionally the eggs of smaller birds.

It is best attracted to feeding stations with a slice of watermelon. evidently irresistible to the Gila Woodpecker.

Nesting begins early in April with the laying of three to five eggs. The male and female share the duties of incubation which usually takes two weeks. It is not yet known how long it takes for chicks to reach flying age. but the adult birds continue to feed their young for several days after they leave the nest.

Gila Woodpeckers do not migrate and will usually raise two. sometimes three broods a year.

Elf Owl

The world's smallest owl makes its spring and summer home in the deserts of Arizona. New Mexico and western Texas. It has also been seen in Nevada and Colorado. but its favorite haunts are among the stands of tall saguaro cactus of Arizona.

With a body only five to six inches (12.7 to 15.2 cm) long. the bird has a surprising 15 inch (38 cm) wingspread. Its lack of ear tufts and short tail help distinguish it from the Pygmy and Ferruginous Owls. And its white 'eyebrows.' round head. yellow eyes and gray underparts help distinguish it from the Flammulated Owl.

Though small in size. the Elf Owl *(Microthene witneyi)* is big of voice. Its whistles and yips. most often heard at nightfall. are loud enough to be confused with the calls of young coyotes.

A night feeder. the Elf Owl favors insects which it often catches with its feet while on the wing. Sometimes it takes its prey on the ground or on flowers or foliage that attract insects. Often it is seen hovering over good hunting spots. waiting for its prey. But it will also hunt from a perch. swooping out for flying insects much like a flycatcher.

When it catches a stinging insect. it removes or crushes the stinger before eating the prey.

For their nests. Elf Owls are entirely dependent on holes dug by Woodpeckers in cactus plants. particularly the saguaro cactus. Most of these holes are the work of the Gila and Gilded Woodpeckers. but the Owls have also been known to nest in holes dug in mesquites. sycamores and dead pines by other Woodpeckers of the region.

The male Owl arrives in the nesting area first and selects a likely nesting hole which he occupies. His calls from within the hole attract the female. Little or nothing is done to line the nest cavity before one to five white eggs are laid. Like most other Owls. the female alone incubates the eggs for the necessary 24 days.

Opposite: The Roadrunner is a ground cuckoo which rarely flies and nests close to the ground in large cacti, shrubs or mesquite bush.

The male, who feeds the female from the time the pair forms, continues bringing food to the nest after the eggs hatch. The female takes the food and gives it to her chicks. It takes 28 to 33 days for the chicks to fly. Like all Owls, Elf Owls raise just one brood a season.

In the fall, the birds leave their summer haunts to move south often into arid regions of northwest Mexico. Many, however, do not cross the border but remain in southern New Mexico and Arizona.

Elf Owls raised in captivity have lived seven years, and there has been at least one pair that bred and raised a chick in captivity.

Roadrunner

A large, terrestrial member of the Cuckoo Family, the Roadrunner of the arid southwest is one of the easiest American birds to recognize.

No other bird in the habitat runs with such speed and agility. Known also as the Chaparral Cock, Ground Cuckoo, Lizard Bird and Snake Killer, it earned its most popular name from the early days of western settlement when it was often seen running ahead of horses and carriages.

It can sustain speeds of 15 miles (24 km) an hour over surprising distances, and by using its short, rounded wings and long tail it can make the abrupt turns necessary to catch lizards and other swift, elusive prey.

Roadrunners are brown above and white, streaked with brown below. In flight, they also show a crescent of white on each wing and white on the tips of the outer feathers of their tails. About half of the bird's over-all 20 to 24 inch (51 to 61 cm) length is tail.

The black, slender beak is about as long as the head. Long, spiked feathers at the top and back of the head form an untidy crest, and like many other members of the Cuckoo or *Cuculidae* Family, Roadrunners have a patch of bare skin behind each eye. The patch fades from pale blue to orange as it approaches the ear opening. The strong legs of most birds are also pale blue.

Although it belongs to a large family with 127 cuckoo species scattered about the world, the Roadrunner is unique to the Western Hemisphere. It is found from

Southern California. east to Kansas and Oklahoma and south into central America. New Mexico has adopted the Roadrunner as its state bird.

Unlike the European cuckoo *(Cuculus canorus)*, which is noted for its parasitic nesting. the Roadrunner *(Geococcyx californianus)* has more respectable domestic habits. Pairs breed for life and they will remain in and defend their hunting territory year-round.

Nests of sticks. snakeskins. leaves. and dried cattle dung are built in the low branches of trees some three to four feet (92 to 122 cm) off the ground. Incubation of the three to five. white to yellowish eggs takes 20 days. Both parents care for the young until they fledge 17 to 19 days after hatching. Two or more pairs have been known to share a nest. but such community nesting is more common among the Ani. another cuckoo species.

There are many exaggerations. typical of western folklore. concerning the Roadrunner. Perhaps the most common tale has it that the bird will use cactus spines to build a trap for rattlesnakes. Although it does not build traps. the Roadrunner can kill gophers. rats. mice. lizards and small snakes. including rattlers. The bulk of its diet. however. is made up on insects. especially crickets. grasshoppers. caterpillars. beetles. bugs and ants.

Hooded Oriole

The birds that Americans call Orioles are actually members of the large Troupial Family which includes blackbirds. cowbirds. grackles and meadowlarks. In all. there are 91 species. all song birds unique to the New World. Twenty-two troupials are seasonal or year-round residents of North America.

True Orioles. found in tropical climates of the Old World. have ten primary wing feathers. Troupials have just nine primaries.

The Hooded Oriole *(Icterus cuculatus)* nests from the arid regions of California. Arizona. New Mexico and Texas south into Mexico. Most birds winter south of the Mexican border.

Like other New World Orioles. it weaves an elaborate nest and has colorful plumage with male birds showing more contrast than females.

The male Hooded Oriole. 7 to 7¾ inches (17.8 to 19.7 cm) long. has a bright. orange-yellow body. black tail. black and white wings. and a black mask which extends down the throat and part way down the breast. The two white wing bars show best when the bird is in flight. The female is pale green above and pale yellow below with gray wings that show two white bars in flight. Young birds look much like females. but young males show a black throat.

In their summer range. the birds are often seen around ranch houses and small towns. They have been known to nest in gardens. but they prefer cottonwoods and syca-

Right: The brightly colored Hooded Oriole can be spotted hunting for food high in the trees.

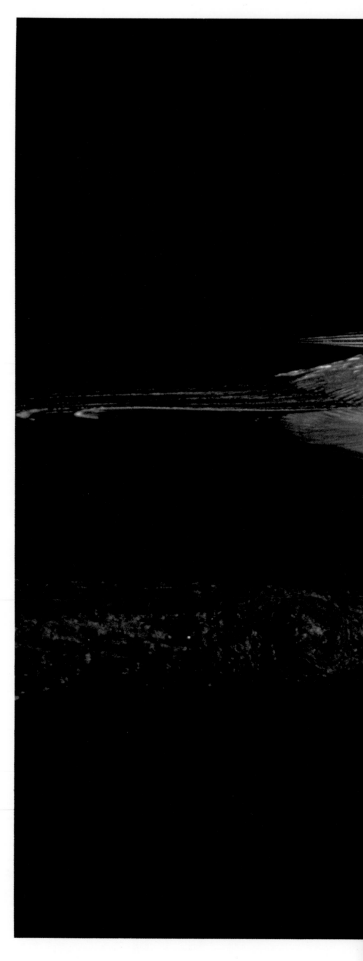

mores that grow on the banks of streams. They also use walnut, cypress, eucalyptus, and palm trees. In fact, where palms are available, the female Hooded Oriole uses palm fibers to weave the cup-shaped, hanging nest.

Where palms are not available, the bird will use palmetto or yucca fibers. The nest is often hidden in a cluster of Spanish moss, mistletoe, or thick foliage.

Male birds usually arrive in the nesting area two or three days ahead of the female. When she arrives, the male begins a courtship display that includes chattering and posturing, bobbing and chasing.

Birds raise two or three broods a season. Thus egg laying may begin as early as April and continue into August. Clutches range from three to five eggs that are pale yellow or blue with spots of brown or gray. Incubation, done solely by the female, takes 12 to 14 days. Chicks leave the nest after 14 days.

Bronzed and Brownheaded Cowbirds, also members of the Troupial Family, practice parasitic nesting and sometimes lay an egg in a Hooded Oriole's nest. The female incubates the egg and raises the chick as one of her own. Because Cowbirds are only slightly bigger, however, the parasite chick does not cause great hardship.

Turkey Vulture

The classic scene of a grotesque Turkey Vulture *(Cathartes aura)* perched on a cactus as it waits for some hapless victim of the desert to succumb to the merciless sun embodies several misconceptions. And worst of all it fails entirely to portray the Vulture in its best element—the sky.

With a maximum wingspan of 72 inches (1.8 m), the bird is king of the air currents. It can circle for hours, rising and falling with the thermals, and never once flap its wings. No other bird is so adept at static soaring.

Sometimes it seems to defy the rules of aerodynamics. I have seen Turkey Vultures glide forward with good speed into winds of 20 to 30 miles an hour without flapping. Although the bird roosts at night and comes to earth to feed, it spends most of the daylight hours aloft, using its keen eyesight and well-developed sense of smell, only recently discovered by science, to hunt for carrion.

Close up, it is true that the Turkey Vulture is not handsome. The dull red to purple of its bare neck and head give this bird its common name, but its strong, down-curved and hooked beak is hardly turkey-like. Looks, however, are just skin deep.

Birds raised from chicks make devoted pets. They enjoy being petted and will follow their benefactors like dogs. After long separation, pet birds have been known to recognize their owners and greet them with affection.

Turkey Vultures are also dutiful parents. After one to three (usually two) eggs are laid on the bare floor of a cave or hollow stump, the parents share incubation duties during the 38 to 41 days it takes for the eggs to hatch. Both work hard at chick feeding which is done by regurgitation of food into the bill where chicks can drink the soupy stuff. After 70 to 80 days, the young birds are ready to fly and begin feeding for themselves.

Another misconception is that Turkey Vultures are restricted to arid regions. Although we place them here with other desert birds in a bow to convention, the Turkey Vulture's range extends from coast to coast and from South

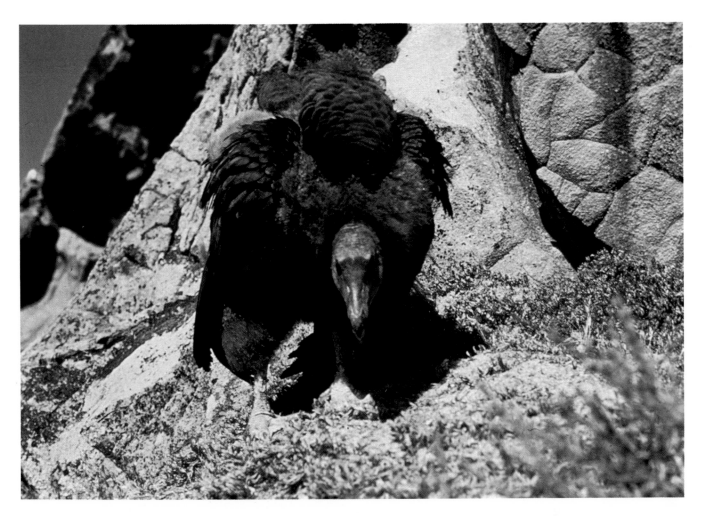

America north into southern Canada. Although not a true migrant, the bird retreats to a winter boundary that follows a rough line from Maryland to Northern California.

While the Turkey Vulture is the most common North American Vulture, two other species of the family *Cathartidae* are found north of the Mexican border. The smaller Black Vulture *(Coragyps atratus)* inhabits both North and South America but because of its preference for warm, tropical climate it rarely ventures into Canada or far west of the Rocky Mountains.

The Californa Condor *(Gymnogyps californianus)* is all but extinct. The 20 to 30 surviving birds occupy preserves in the rugged mountains of California's Ventura and Santa Barbara counties. This condor's wingspread of 9½ feet (2.9 m) makes it the largest North American landbird, but it will not be with us much longer.

Regarded as a living fossil, the condor reached its peak population about one million years ago during the Pleistocene epoch when large animals roamed the continent. Even a century ago, when western cattle ranches afforded an abundance of large carcasses, the condor flourished from Canada to Mexico. But today, it seems that efforts to save the huge bird are doomed.

When adult birds, even in favorable times of ample food and isolation, raise but one chick every other year, it is fair to say that the California Condor is headed for sure extinction.

Opposite: Turkey Vultures raise their young as a couple in sheltered places, but do not build a nest.
Above: It takes nearly a year for a young Condor to fly well and five to six years to begin breeding.

The four other members of the Vulture family are residents of Central or South America. They are the King Vulture, the Yellow-headed Vulture, the Greater Yellow-headed Vulture, and the Andean Condor. The latter, with a wingspread of 10 feet (3.04 m) is the world's largest bird of prey. There are no Vultures in the Old World.

Because they scavange dead animals that would otherwise stink and breed vermin, all members of the Vulture Family are regarded as beneficial birds. Although the Turkey Vulture has been known to kill young herons, ibises, newborn pigs and even eat pumpkins when starving, its main diet is the dead flesh of many animals, ranging from alligators to such common victims of highway traffic as opossums, raccoons, rabbits, snakes and skunks.

Its ability to locate hidden carrion, helped ornithologist K E Stager prove in the 1960s that, contrary to traditional belief, birds can smell, and that the Turkey Vulture has a very sharp nose. Most other vultures, surprisingly, have a limited sense of smell. Black Vultures, in fact, often rely on Turkey Vultures to find carrion. When the Turkey Vultures drop down to feed, the Black Vultures follow and often drive the larger birds away.

WESTERN MOUNTAINS

The Rockies, Cascades, Sierra Nevada and other lofty mountains of the American west are largely forested with firs, pines and, in some select regions, the renowned Sequoias and Redwoods.

There is, however, great variety and complexity in the vegetation and animals of the high elevations. The variety and complexity is well reflected in the bird life.

The bird populations of the mountains are related closely to the populations of the boreal forests, but the mountains have a dimension the boreal regions lack. It is elevation.

The Clark's Nutcracker rarely nests below 6,000 feet (1,829 m) or above 8,000 feet (2,438 m). The Bantailed Pigeon prefers to nest in the foothills where hardwoods, particularly oaks, provide the bird's favorite food.

Many species from the Dipper to the Red-tailed Hawk migrate vertically, moving to lower elevations in the winter and returning to the heights in the summer. Others, such as the Brown Creeper, seem as happy in the snow as they are in spring verdure.

In other cases, the levels have apparently acted as barriers. The Chestnut-backed Chickadee, for instance, dwells in the forested coastal mountains, but in the lower northern forests its environmental niche is filled by the Boreal Chickadee.

Similar relationships can be found with eastern bird populations. The multi-colored Mountain Tanager has an eastern counterpart in the Scarlet Tanager. The Steller's Jay and the Scrub Jay of the west, though closely related to the Blue Jay of the east, do not cross boundary lines. Then there is the strange case of the Lewis Woodpecker that has developed in its isolation the ability to catch insects on the wing, something other woodpeckers do not do.

Thus the Western Mountains present a unique environment with a unique bird population.

Right: The Red-naped Sapsucker (*Sphyrapicus varius*), a member of the woodpecker family which dwells in the Rocky Mountains, is characterized by its red nape, forehead and throat (only partly red in the female). Sapsuckers feed on insects in tree bark, but they also bore for the tree sap which they like.
Opposite top: The Red-shafted Flicker (*Colaptes auratus*), a red-mustached common flicker, resides in the western woodlands. It provides the useful service of boring holes in trees to be used by other birds for nesting.
Opposite bottom: Like all sapsuckers, the Yellow-bellied Sapsucker (a subspecies of *Sphyrapicus varius*) has a white rump, barred back and a long, white wing patch.

Clark's Nutcracker

All members of the Crow or *Corvidae* Family—ravens, jays, magpies, nutcrackers and crows themselves—are characterized by a high level of intelligence and great adaptability.

The family is well represented around the world. Ravens are at home even in the Arctic. Although the family probably originated in the Old World, it was an early New World migrant. Fossils of crow-like birds found in Colorado are 12 million years old.

Crows can be taught to count and solve puzzles. They have surprising memories, and they can mimic almost any sound, including calls of most other birds and the human voice.

The Clark's Nutcracker *(Nucifraga columbiana),* a resident of the Sierra Nevada and the Rockies, needs its well-developed memory to survive. The bird stores nuts and seeds in hundreds of caches during the growing season. When winter comes, it finds its stored food even though it might be covered with snow.

Named for Captain William Cook of the 1803-06 Lewis and Clark Expedition through the Northwest, the bird itself is a curious adventurer. It will come into mountain camps to steal food or beg handouts. Sometimes it even goes into tents or cabins. Imitating bird calls, particularly the hoots of owls, will usually bring several Nutcrackers out of the trees to investigate.

The bird, 12 to 13 inches (30.5 to 33 cm) long, has a gray body and black wings and tail. White wing patches are conspicuous when the bird is at rest or in flight. On the ground it may either hop or walk with a jerky gait. It can cling to the sides of trees and sometimes pecks at bark, searching for insects and giving an excellent imitation of a woodpecker.

Its main food is pine nuts which it pries from cones with its strong bill. It eats the nuts, shell and all, or else stores them in its throat for deposit in a food cache. Some birds have been known to have established more than a thousand caches in one season.

With a variety of flight patterns, a Clark's will sometimes flap steadily for straight flight like a jay, sometimes undulate its flight with intermittent flaps like a woodpecker, and other times make spectacular, folded-wing dives into deep canyons. It brakes the dives by suddenly extending its wings to make an explosive *wooosh* in the air.

Nest building by both sexes can begin as early as February when the nesting trees are still laden with snow. Made of twigs and bark and lined with pine needles or grass, the nest is 11 to 12 inches (27.9 to 30 cm) in diameter. Two to three pale green to grayish green eggs are laid as early as March, and the birds may be forced to incubate them during snowstorms.

The eggs hatch after 17 or 18 days, and young birds can fly 24 to 28 days after hatching.

Below and opposite: The Clark's Nutcracker lives high in the pine-covered mountain ranges. Its population size fluctuates with the yield of pine seeds, which it stores temporarily under its tongue in cheek pouches.

Below: The Band-tailed Pigeon has been emerging from the forests and adjusting to urban and city life.
Left: This female is the last of the once prolific Passenger Pigeons, photographed shortly before she died at age 29 in the Cincinnati Zoological Gardens.
Opposite: A city bird, the Rock Dove is the pigeon commonly seen on city streets and in the parks.

Band-tailed Pigeon

The Band-tailed Pigeon *(Columba fasciata)* of western forests was almost hunted to extinction, but today, thanks to protection, flocks are making a comeback. There are two nesting groups, one in the Pacific states north into British Columbia, and the other in the Rocky Mountain highlands of New Mexico, Arizona, Colorado and Utah. In winter the birds move to lower elevations and southern latitudes. Some winter in the highlands of Central South America where they are still hunted without restriction.

The Band-tail, 14 to 15½ inches (35.6 to 39.4 cm) long, has the heavy build of a Rock Dove or Street Pigeon *(Columba livia)* but it is slightly larger with more solid coloring. The Band-tail is generally blue-gray with a dark band next to a white tail border. The white and dark markings are most obvious when the bird is in flight. Adults also have a thin band of white across the backs of their necks.

The birds migrate in flocks, arriving in their nesting grounds in March, April, and May. They eat wild berries, seeds and nuts, with a preference for acorns. They also eat

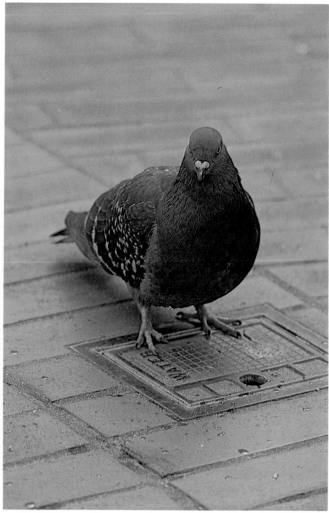

Above both and opposite: These Rock Doves are typical examples of the common coloring of this species. Other Street Pigeons may have plumage ranging from white to brown-red, slate black, and piebald.

insects. They sometimes feed on the ground, but usually they pick berries, seeds and nuts directly from the limbs.

Nests are rough platforms of sticks and twigs some 8 inches (20.3 cm) across. They might be from 8 to 40 feet (2.44 to 12.2 m) up in either conifers or hardwood trees.

The egg laying season lasts from May to July in most of the breeding range, but birds in Arizona and New Mexico might have eggs as late as October. One, sometimes two eggs, are laid. Incubation by both birds takes 18 to 20 days, and chicks can fly about a month after hatching.

Band-tails utter a deep *whoo* that is often mistaken for an owl's call, but pigeons are not nocturnal callers or flyers. Flocks, however, are often seen at dusk, flying at tree top level as they return to a favored roost.

Of all the stories told by New World settlers there could hardly be any that challenged belief more than the accounts of vast flocks of pigeons that darkened the sky for hours in their northward flights.

Alexander Wilson (1766-1813), one of the first to attempt a count, said that one flock, a mile (1.6 km) wide,

and flying tier upon tier so thickly that it darkened the sky, took four hours to pass on its northern flight. He estimated that the flock contained 2¼ billion birds. In 1866, W Ross King watched a flight near the Ontario border that he believed was a mile (1.6 km) wide and 300 miles (483 km) long. It took 14 hours to pass.

At night, the birds would perch in trees in such numbers that their weight would break limbs up to two feet (61 cm) in diameter. John James Audubon (1785 to 1851) reported that forests appeared to have been struck by hurricanes after the pigeons had departed.

These were Passenger Pigeons *(Ectopistes migratorius).* With a population once estimated at 3 to 5 billion in the US alone, there was probably no other bird in the world as numerous.

It no longer exists. The last Passenger Pigeon died in captivity in 1914. Although clearing of forests took a toll, the main cause for extinction was excessive hunting. Commercial hunters throughout the late 1800s shot and netted the birds by the thousands. In one month, netters reportedly took 700,000 birds from a colony in Michigan. Protection for the Passenger Pigeon did not come until too late.

Other North American members of the Pigeon or *Colombidae* Family, reckoned at 16 doves and pigeons, have also been heavily hunted, but they survived.

Dipper

There are three other Dipper species in the world, but just one other lives in the Americas. It is the White-capped or White-headed Dipper of the Andes. Although related to wrens and thrushes, Dippers have highly developed preening glands, about ten times bigger than the average songbird's, which they need to oil their plumage frequently for their underwater food hunting.

Dippers are believed to have earned their name from their habit of bobbing several times a second when perched by the side of a stream.

Picture a song bird that can fly underwater and you will begin to appreciate the unusual Dipper or Water Ouzel (*Cinclus mexicanus*) of the North American west.

Its habitat is the swift mountain stream, and its range extends from Alaska south into Mexico. Both sexes have a plumage of dark gray. Legs are pale pink, and the sharp beak is black at the tip fading to light gray at the base. A line of white on the upper eyelid is pronounced on some birds, but too faint to notice on most. The Dipper is 7 to 8.5 inches (17.8 to 21.6 cm) long.

Above: This Dipper is peculiarly adapted to fly through water and to 'dip' into streams to pluck out its prey.
Opposite: Red-tailed Hawks keep rodent numbers down.

With unwebbed feet, the Dipper is a slow surface swimmer, but when it dives underwater, it uses its wings to swim and has no trouble advancing against strong currents. It also walks underwater, using its claws to grip water-smoothed rocks.

Its diet is made up chiefly of the larvae of various water insects, water beetles, and water bugs. Occasionally it will eat snails, clams, and trout fry. Sometimes it will wash food before feeding it to its chicks.

In summer it may range as high as the timberline, more than 11,000 feet (3,353 m) in some mountains. Although not a true migrant, it is forced by frozen streams to move to lower elevations in winter.

Dippers sing throughout the year with a clear series of wren-like notes that can often be heard above the roar of rapids or falls.

The female builds a nest of moss and grass on a river rock or ledge that is often damp with spray. The nest, about a foot (30 cm) in diameter, has a dome shape and a side entrance that makes it look like an old fashioned oven. When nesting begins, both male and female aggressively chase other Dippers from their territory.

The white eggs, usually four or five of them, can be laid as early as March at low elevations. The female incubates the eggs until they hatch in 15 to 17 days. Young leave the nest when they are 24 or 25 days old.

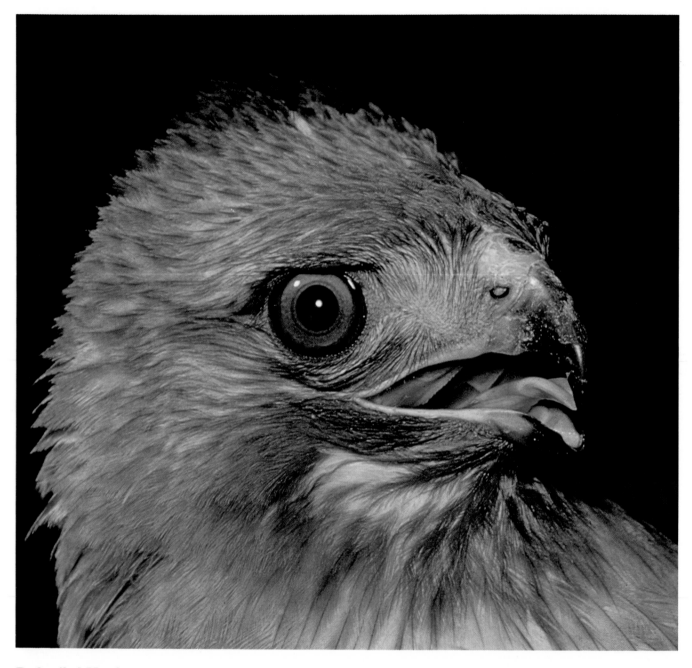

Red-tailed Hawk

With a nesting range extending from Panama and the West Indies into northern Canada and Alaska, the Red-tailed Hawk *(Buteo jamaicensis)* is the best known and most widely distributed hawk in North America.

Its large size and buff red tail feathers also make it one of the easiest hawks to identify. Adult birds are 19 to 25 inches (48.2 to 63.5 cm) long and have a wingspread of 46 to 58 inches (116.8 to 147.3 cm). They are dark brown above and mostly white below, but there is a dark band of streaks running across the belly. Plumage of some specimens, particularly in the west, may be more black than brown, but a red tail remains the distinctive identifying feature.

The Red-tail's cry is a prolonged, high pitched *kreee-ee-e,* often uttered as it leaves its tree top perch on a hunting

Above: A young Red-tailed Hawk.
Opposite: The largest of its genus, the Ferruginous Hawk *(Buteo regalis)* dwells in open prairie country or in badlands, feeding on prairie dogs and ground squirrels.

sortie. The hawk preys on a wide variety of rodents, small birds, and reptiles. It can kill rattlesnakes and copperheads, but there are cases on record where the Red-tail has been bitten and died of the venom after killing the snake.

Red-tailed Hawks prefer mixed country of open fields and forests, but they can be seen in mountains, deserts, prairies, and settled farmland. They are rare, however, where there are large tracts of unbroken forest.

Many birds remain in their nesting range year-round, but others, particularly young birds, fly south or move to lower elevations in the autumn. Red-tails are seen with many other species during Pennsylvania's famous Hawk

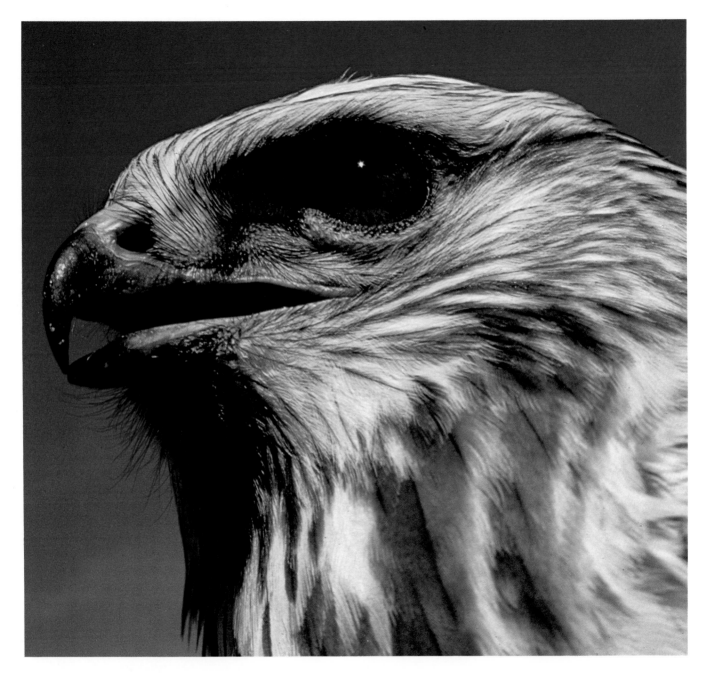

Mountain migration flights. Recent counts, however, suggest that the number of Red-tails is declining.

Though more adaptable than any other hawk, Red-tailed Hawks, like others, have suffered from loss of habitat. Recent studies also suggest that egg shell thinning due to pesticides in prey, may be contributing to the decline.

Pairs are believed to mate for life. The courtship flight, often reaching great altitudes, is a sham battle. The male dives on the female who flips over to project her talons and sometimes catch the male bird. These flights can occur any time of year, but during mating season, they end with the birds gliding to a tree-top perch where they copulate.

Their nest, built of twigs, sticks and sprigs of pine or fir are 2.5 to three feet (76.2 to 91.4 cm) in diameter. Often it will be built in the tallest oak or conifer at the edge of a grove, and may be anywhere from 15 to about 70 feet (4.6 to 21.3 m) above the ground.

Red-tails have two to three white eggs spotted with brown. The laying season can start as early as February in southern regions. The female, fed by the male, incubates the eggs. They hatch after about 30 days, and young fly some 45 days after hatching.

Lewis' Woodpecker

The Lewis's Woodpecker *(Melanerpes lewis)*, common in western mountains particularly between elevations of 2,000 and 9,000 feet (610 and 2,743 m), behaves more like a flycatcher than a woodpecker.

It does nest in tree cavities, perch vertically on the sides of tree trunks, and pick up insects from bark with its sharp beak, but it usually takes insects on the fly. Sometimes it will stay in the air swooping and turning much like a swallow to catch and eat flying insects. Other times it will hunt

from a perch, swooping down like a bluebird to catch its prey and then returning to eat it on its perch.

Like the Clark's Nutcracker, the Lewis' Woodpecker was discovered during the Lewis and Clark Expedition (1803-1806), the species being named for Meriwether Lewis.

The bird, 10½ to 11½ inches (26.7 to 29.2 cm) long, is best recognized by its solid black back. Most other woodpeckers of the same size have bars or patches of white on their backs. The brownish-red of the face blends into a rather wide collar of dull white. Males and females have similar plumage, but the male is slightly larger and has a longer bill.

Unlike other members of the family *Picadae*, Lewis' Woodpeckers rarely drum on trees, and their flight, rather than undulating, is usually smooth with regular wing beats. Although insects are its main food, the Lewis' Woodpecker will sometimes eat fruit and consequently draws the wrath of orchard growers. By preying on harmful insects, however, the bird certainly is beneficial in the balance.

It is believed that the male, with the larger beak, does most of the excavation for the nest. It is usually carved in dead trees, but sometimes a living tree is selected. The entrance, 2 to 3 inches (5.1 to 7.6 cm) in diameter, leads to a cavity 9 to 30 inches (22.9 to 76.2 cm) deep. Sometimes the birds will use a nesting cavity abandoned by some other bird, particularly a Flicker.

Egg laying season begins as early as May and continues into August with a good deal of regional variation. Six or seven white eggs make up the normal clutch. They take 12 or 13 days to hatch, and young birds fly 28 to 34 days after hatching. Both birds incubate the eggs and feed the young.

The bird, also called Black Woodpecker or Crow Woodpecker, ranges into western Canada, east to South Dakota and Texas, and south into Mexico. Strays wander all the way to Massachusetts, but their appearance there is always a big event.

Chestnut-backed Chickadee

Always busy searching trees for insects, chickadees show little fear of man. They often move through a forest in flocks of 15 or more, chirping and tweeting briskly as they feed.

The Chestnut-backed Chickadee *(Parus rufescens)* belongs to the Titmouse or *Paridae* Family. There are 65 species worldwide, 14 of which, including titmice, bushtits, chickadees, and the verdin, are found in North America.

There are five other North American chickadees, and although they can be seen anywhere there are dense groves of trees, two species of chickadee are rarely seen together. This is because competition for insects makes it difficult for them to co-exist. Chickadees are thus separated geographically.

Opposite: A Red-tailed Hawk displays its distinctive tail.
Below: Threse Peregrine Falcon *(Falco peregrinus)* chicks belong to a protected species which is being bred in captivity to increase its seriously reduced numbers.

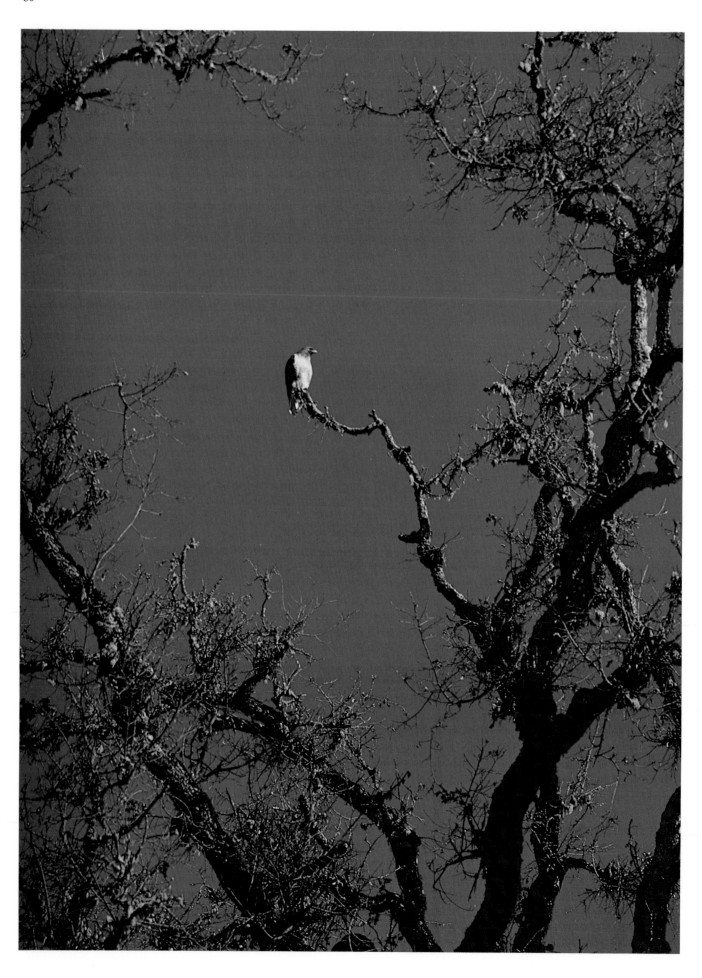

The Chestnut-backed Chickadee's primary range is a narrow strip of forest running from Alaska south through the coastal mountains to central California. Some inland flocks, however, live in the mountains of Idaho and Montana.

Chickadees in their restless search for insects do not hesitate to invade urban gardens or city parks. A flock seems to work in a tree, crawling over limbs, twigs, and leaves, until the supply of insects is exhausted. Then the birds progress to a neighboring tree without pause.

Chickadees can withstand cold temperatures and do not migrate great distances. Some flocks, however, do move to lower elevations during winter months.

The Chestnut-backed Chickadee, from 4½ to 5 inches (11.4 to 12.7 cm) long, has white cheeks which contrast sharply with a black chest, brown cap, and rusty brown or chestnut back and rump. Male and female are alike.

The bird does not have a whistling call like other chickadees but it keeps up a steady conversation with its high pitched *tseeks, dees,* and *chics.*

Chestnut-backs nest from March to June, usually selecting a natural cavity or a woodpecker hole in a tree. Some pairs, however, will carve their own cavity in a dead fir. Mosses, animal hairs and feathers are used to line the nest.

About six or seven white eggs dotted with rusty brown are laid. Incubation period is not known exactly, but it is probably less than two weeks. It is also not known when young birds leave the nest, but it is likely about 18 days after hatching like other chickadees.

Brown Creeper

Seen in forested mountains throughout North America, the Brown Creeper *(Certhia familiaris)* is the only representative of its family seen in both the Old and New Worlds.

Known in the British Isles as the Tree Creeper, the bird uses its stiff tail feathers as props as it works its way up trunks and out branches in a restless search for insects. It can move vertically and even upside down with ease, but it either cannot or will not work downward. Typically, the Brown Creeper moves from the base of a tree, often in a spiral path, until it reaches a top branch. Then it will fly to the base of another tree and start again.

Nuthatches with similar coloration and feeding habits, work both up and down with equal ease.

The Brown Creeper is 5 to 5¾ inches (12.7 to 14.60 cm) long. It has a narrow body and thin, down-curved bill. A nuthatch's bill is straight and much shorter. Creepers are brown with some white streaks or speckles above, and white below. There is a white eyebrow line, and the tail and rump are often rufus. Plumage is the same for both sexes.

Opposite: Red-tailed Hawks will often perch for hours, waiting to swoop on unsuspecting prey.
Right: The home of the Brown Creeper is the mature coniferous forest, where it nests under loose bark.

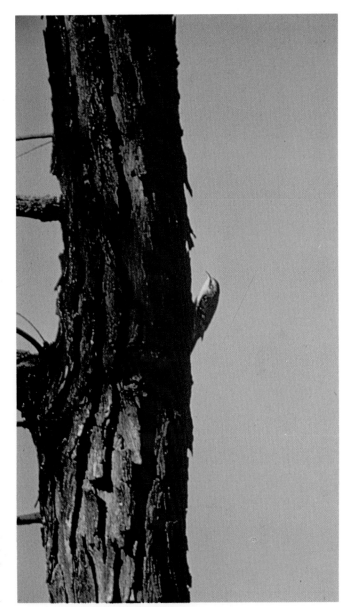

Although it usually feeds alone, it is sometimes seen with other small birds, including its closest relatives, the titmice and nuthatches.

Its predominant song is a whispered *tzzz* or occasionally a prolonged *zzzz-zt.* When nesting, the song becomes more varied, almost melodious.

Though many birds remain in their nesting range there is considerable seasonal migration. In summer, Brown Creepers can be seen in subarctic forests from central Alaska across Canada to Newfoundland. In winter, many birds retreat to more southern forests of the United States and Mexico.

The nest, a hammock of moss, bark, and twigs with feather lining, is shaped like a crescent. From March to July, depending on climate, five or six white eggs, with pale brown spots, are laid. Incubation takes about two weeks, and young begin to fly another two weeks after hatching.

Other names include California Creeper, Sierra Creeper, Rocky Mountain Creeper and Mexican Creeper.

PRAIRIES

The central plains of North America, once a seemingly endless grassland dominated by huge herds of buffalo, have seen profound changes since pioneer times.

Much of the grass has been plowed under. The wild herds of buffalo are no more. Populations of many birds, such as the Prairie Chicken, have declined drastically. But generally birds have adjusted to the changes with greater success than animals.

It must be said that the prairie lacks the variety of species found in the western mountains or the eastern woodlands. But the birds of the prairie fit remarkably well into the special features of their environment.

The region, west of the Mississippi and east of the Rocky Mountains, extends from the Gulf Coast of Texas well into central Canada. It is a flat landscape, devoid of hills or many trees, but there are rivers, streams, and ponds.

Thus the birds of the prairie are mostly ground feeders and ground nesters. Because singing of territorial or courtship songs from a tree-top is impossible, many birds such as the Longspur, Lark Bunting and Horned Lark sing their songs in flight. And both song and flight can be spectacular.

There is no lack of predators, including sharp-eyed birds of prey such as the Rough-legged Hawk, and the ground dwellers have learned to hide their nest cleverly. The Western Meadowlark often builds a dome of grass which is extremely difficult to find. Some birds decoy enemies away from their nests with a broken-wing act which the Killdeer particularly has refined to a high art.

In winter, most birds depart migrating far to the south or at least to the southern portion of the plain, leaving much of the prairie cold, bleak and silent.

Redwing Blackbird

For sheer numbers, the Redwing Blackbird ranks high among North American songbirds. One winter flock in Dismal Swamp, Virginia, was estimated at 15 million birds.

The Redwing Blackbird *(Agelaius phoeniceus)* can be found almost anywhere on marshy ground from the Pacific to the Atlantic. The bird is 7 to 9½ inches (17.9 to 24.1 cm) long, and has a wingspread of 12 to 14½ inches (30.5 to 36.8 cm).

The male is jet black except for bright red shoulder patches that sometimes have a lower border of yellow. Females are brown above and streaked light and brown below. They have a light streak over each eye.

Left: Flocks of blackbirds, including Redwings, descend on farmers' fields, eating up grain and harmful insects.

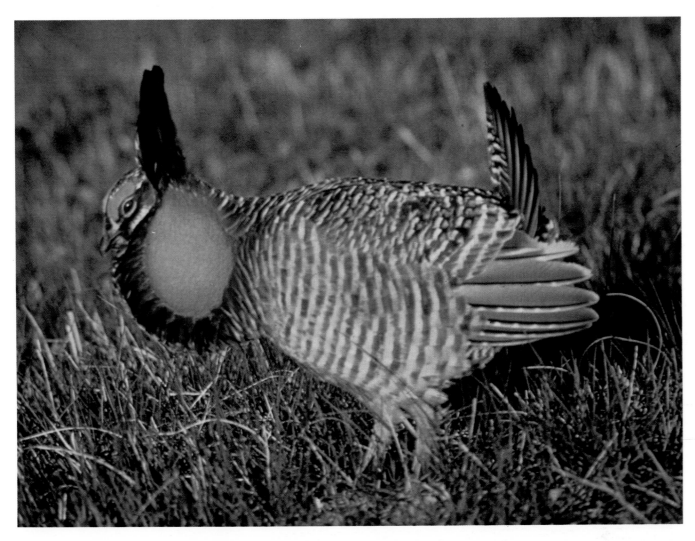

Opposite: A Redwing at home among the reeds.
Above: A Greater Prairie Chicken displays its plumage.

Redwings like slow moving water where reeds grow thickly, and banks are covered with low trees or bushes. They will range into upland fields and meadows for food, but they rarely stray far from water.

In winter, many Redwings move north into the subarctic from the Yukon across Canada to Nova Scotia. In winter, the birds retreat into the southern United States.

At the start of northern migrations in February and March, the males lead the females by several days. Upon arrival at the breeding ground, the male selects a territory and defends it by singing from a high perch. The song is a liquid *onk-a-reee* or *o-kwa-eeee* and often ends in a squeak or *chack*.

Any invaders are chased away fiercely. Redwings will attack much larger birds, including ospreys, ravens and crows. They are sometimes seen riding the back of a crow, pecking wildly.

Redwings are ground feeders and eat seeds, insects and occasionally snails or berries. About three-fourths of their diet is vegetable matter and about a fourth animal matter.

Also known as the Swamp Blackbird and Marsh Blackbird, the Redwing lives up to these names by building its nest in cattails, bushes or trees next to or over the water. Woven loosely of cattails or other fibers and lined with grasses, the nest is big enough to hold about four pale green or blue, spotted eggs.

Incubation by the female takes 11 or 12 days. Young are able to leave the nest after ten days and climb among twigs or reeds, but a few days more growth is needed before they can fly.

Like the Western Meadowlark, Redwing Blackbirds belong to the Troupial Family which includes cowbirds, parasite nesters that sometimes leave their eggs in the Redwing's nest.

Greater Prairie Chicken

The Greater Prairie Chicken, once common in central Canada and the northern plain states, is now found only in parts of Illinois, Michigan and Wisconsin. Its numbers are still declining.

The bird's eastern counterpart, the Heath Hen, is extinct, and a subspecies, the Attwater's Prairie Chicken today numbers no more than 2,000 individuals confined to a small range spanning the border of Louisiana and Texas.

Once prized as a game bird, the Prairie Chicken's undoing was not the gun but the plow. Since it is a leaf, stem,

The popular, outgoing Western Meadowlark, the state bird of Montana, is well known for its melodious voice and for its variety of songs.

seed and insect eater, the Greater Prairie Chicken *(Tympanuchus cupido)* can find little nourishment on plowed land.

The bird is 16½ to 18 inches (41.9 to 45.7 cm) long. Its plumage is barred dark brown and buff with the barring on the belly being more uniform and more widely spaced than the barring on the back. The rounded tail is solidly dark for the male and barred for the female. The light throat and upper neck is bordered on each side by a dark line of feathers running from each eye down the side of the neck. The brown head has a small crest and there is a bare patch of skin over each eye.

Male birds show neck sacks of orange skin that they inflate during courtship. Females have only small patches on the neck.

The closely related Lesser Prairie Chicken has similar markings and feeding habits, but the smaller bird is found in more arid regions. Surviving flocks are in Kansas, New Mexico, Oklahoma and Texas.

Prairie chickens are insect eaters from May through October when the grasshopper, its favorite delicacy, is prevalent. In other seasons, the birds concentrate entirely on plant food, including fruit, leaves, flowers, shoots and seeds.

The nesting season begins in April or May when the female selects a hollow beneath grasses or weeds or under a low bush. She lines her well-concealed nest with grass before laying about 10 to 12 spotted brown and olive eggs.

Incubation, then, takes 23 or 24 days, and chicks can leave the nest a few hours after hatching. First flights occur one to two weeks after the chicks hatch.

Although Prairie Chickens usually raise just one brood a year, they will make a fresh start with a new clutch of eggs if the first nest should be destroyed.

Lesser Prairie Chickens have similar nesting habits except that they begin about a month later than the Greater Prairie Chicken. Both these representatives of the grouse Family are listed on the Threatened Wildlife List by the United States Office of Endangered Species.

Horned Lark

There are 75 species of song birds that make up the Lark Family, but just one, the Horned Lark *(Eremophila alpestris),* is a legitimate resident of North America.

The Skylark *(Alauda arvensis),* famous songster of the Old World, was introduced on New York's Long Island in the 1880s and later on Vancouver Island in British Colombia. Urbanization eliminated the Long Island flock, but the Vancouver flock has prospered and spread into the state of Washington. Still, its numbers are limited.

What about meadowlarks? Although they are a ground bird and have a plaintive, whistling, song, meadowlarks along with blackbirds, grackles, cowbirds and orioles, belong to the Troupial Family. They are not larks at all.

The Horned Lark, 7 to 8 inches (17.8 to 20.3 cm) long, is generally white below and dark gray to black above. It has a black band or collar high on the breast, a black 'moustache' that runs above the bill and curves downward below the eyes, and a black crown accented by two projecting feathers or 'horns' above and slightly behind the eyes. Females have duller marking than males and lack a clearly defined crown.

A common sight in plowed or unplowed fields, Horned Larks often start their eastern flights in large flocks while snow is still on the ground. Some birds reach the Arctic Coast where they may join colonies of Snow Buntings. Most larks, however, do not migrate so far, and in the southern plain states, many birds winter in their nesting range.

The Horned Lark's flight and song is almost as spectacular as the Skylark's. The Horned Lark does not begin singing until it has climbed to a level 270 to 800 feet (82.3 to 243.8 m) above the ground where it begins flying in a wide circle. Its whistling song sounds like *pit-wee, wee-pit, pit-wee.* Most common single note sounds like *zeet.* It ends its song with a sudden, folded-wing plunge to earth.

Also known as the Prairie Lark, Spring Bird and Wheat Bird, the Horned Lark is most often seen walking or running along the ground as it feeds on seeds and insects.

The nest, built by the female, is a ground hollow lined with grass, hair, plant, or feathers. The nesting season, depending on latitude, ranges from February to July. Usually four pale green eggs are laid. The female alone incubates them for the necessary 11 days. Young can fly nine to twelve days after hatching.

Western Meadowlark

Its double-syllabled call sounds like the wistful notes of a flute, and it is a call you have probably heard often even though you may live thousands of miles from the American prairie.

For the makers of the Hollywood Western, the call has become a handy cliche. A few notes on the soundtrack helps establish the scene—a vast grassland soon to be crossed by the creaking wheels of covered wagons, or the stampeding buffalo, or the Indian brave, or the cowboy.

Ironically the significance of the call to early American ornithologists was overlooked. For the call set the Western Meadowlark *(Sturnella neglecta)* apart from its more brightly colored relative, the Eastern Meadowlark *(Sturnella magna).*

Until about 80 years ago, both birds were thought to be variations of the same species, one of several members of the Troupial Family. When it was discovered, however, that the eastern bird was limited to a whistling *tzing-o-air* that lacked the richness of the western bird's fluting, it was decided to classify the birds as separate species.

Both inhabit grassy fields where they are ground feeders, living on grasshoppers, caterpillars, weevils, plant scales and many other insects that are harmful to crops.

Both select natural depressions in the ground for nest sites and use grass stems, leaves, animal hair and other plant material to build cup-like nests. Sometimes the nest will be completely domed and have a small side entrance.

The Killdeer.

Outwardly, the two species are similar. Both are 8 to 11 inches (20.3 to 27.9 cm) long. They are streaked with various shades of brown above, and have a yellow breast broken by a black V. Outer tail feathers are white which show up well against the brown central feathers. As a general rule, however, the Eastern Meadowlark's plumage is brighter and richer than the Western Meadowlark's.

The Western Meadowlark once ranged from the Pacific states to the eastern limits of the prairie only. Lately, however, with clearing of land, the Western Meadowlark has enlarged its range to overlap the Eastern Meadowlark's range which extends from the Atlantic to the Mississippi Valley.

The male Western Meadowlark usually claims a springtime territory of some seven acres. His song keeps other males away and attracts females, and sometimes more than one female will mate with a male. Nesting season, governed by climate, runs from April to August. Usually five white eggs marked with brown are laid. Incubation takes about two weeks. Both adults feed the chicks until they leave the nest some 12 days after hatching.

Killdeer

Several traits set the Killdeer *(Charadrius vociferus)* apart from other Plovers. It is a shorebird that will wander far from the shore. As its Latin name suggests, it is much noisier than any of the 13 other North American Plovers. And its shrill cry, which is best handled phonetically as *killdeer,* is of course, responsible for its common name.

Migratory tendencies are not as strong in Killdeers as in other Plovers, and in the southern states most birds remain in their nesting area year-round. The Killdeer does, however, have typical Plover markings.

The bird, 9 to 11 inches (22.9 to 27.9 cm) long, is brownish-gray above, with rump and tail coverlets tending toward rufous. Except for two black breast bars, it is white

below. The slim, black bill is shorter than head-length, a typical Plover feature. Sexes are the same size with similar plumage.

Although sometimes seen in flocks of 50, the Killdeer usually flies and feeds alone. It will run some distance and then stand still as if looking or listening for insects. Then it will peck suddenly at the ground when it spots its prey. Insects make up about 98 percent of the Killdeer's diet.

It can be seen hunting on dry fields, meadows, suburban lawns and riverbanks. Freshly plowed fields, however, seem to be highest on its priority of feeding grounds.

Migratory Killdeers are among the first shorebirds to be seen in the northern states and southern Canada. Some begin their northern flights as early as February.

Nests are made on bare ground whether it be a grassy field or a gravel path. Killdeer nests have even been found on the rough gravel between railroad ties. Usually four light gray eggs blotched with brown or black are laid between March and July in southern latitudes and April and July further north.

Incubation, done by both birds, takes 24 days. Although chicks leave the nest soon after hatching and follow their parents in the search for food, they are unable to fly until about 25 days old.

Parent birds are well known for their 'crippled bird act', which is performed to draw an enemy away from a nest or chicks. Killdeers will do this act before dogs, cats, foxes, man or any other threat imaginable. I have seen them flap and hop before the advancing wheels of a tractor as they vainly try to save a hidden nest.

Other names include Pasture Bird, Chattering Plover, Noisy Plover and Field Plover.

Cedar Waxwing

The most nomadic of songbirds, waxwings apparently have a lost heritage. Ornithologists believe they may be the only relics of a large bird group that has vanished. Just three species remain, and two of them, the Bohemian Waxwing *(Bombycilla garrulus)* and the Cedar Waxwing *(Bombycilla cedrorum)* are found in North America.

Bohemians wander through the northern regions of Europe as well, but the Cedar is uniquely American.

The bird, 6½ to 8 inches (16.5 to 20.3 cm) long, is very dapper. Its silky body plumage is golden brown. It wears a black mask and has a tail tipped with a yellow band. Its sharp crest is usually held low to the contour of the head to give the impression of a rakish cap.

The bird's fancy garb is accented by red, wax-like tips on the ends of the secondary wing feathers. These tips, which give the bird its name, are actually extensions of the feather shafts. How these extensions evolved or what their functions may have been remains unknown.

Bohemian Waxwings are generally darker. They lack light bellies but have white and yellow wing patterns.

Waxwings are berry and fruit eaters, and their wanderings seem to be controlled almost entirely by the ripening schedules of their food. Flocks will stay in a garden until

An alert Killdeer is ready to pounce on any insect which comes to view. This robin-sized bird is found all across the temperate regions of North America, in pastures, fields and meadows as well as on the coasts and the inland shores.

Above: Cedar Waxwings gorge themselves on berries when available. but are forced to turn to flycatching when their regular food source runs out.
Opposite: In snowy regions the Rough-legged Hawk shares its territory with the Red-tailed Hawk.

the last berry is plucked. Then they vanish. not to reappear again for a year or perhaps two or even three years later.

Sometimes. after gorging on a crop of berries. they can barely fly. They have also been known to become drunk from eating over-ripe berries that have fermented on the vine or bush. Drunk or sober. they utter a high chirp when they feed.

Sometimes a group of Cedar Waxwings will line up on a limb and pass a berry from beak to beak. Often the berry will travel back and forth more than once before a bird swallows it. Then another berry must be found before the game can resume. In courtship. a pair may pass an insect or flower petal back and forth.

Efforts to find some migratory pattern for Cedar Waxwings have been unsatisfactory. The birds defend no territory until they begin to nest. Even nesting does not follow a predictable schedule. but it is usually late in the summer. It might occur in southeast Alaska. New England or the plains states. There is. however. a southern retreat in the winter by some birds. They have been seen on berry bushes in the West Indies and along the northern coast of South America.

The nests may be built in any kind of tree or shrub at heights ranging from 6 to 50 feet (1.8 to 15.4 m). Sometimes colonies of 12 pairs or more will occupy one tree. Nests. usually built of twigs. weed stems. moss lichen and pine needles. are sometimes lined with yarn taken from the hands of humans. Generally. Cedar Waxwings show little

fear of man or woman. They have been known to pull hair from a woman's head.

Usually three to five pale blue or gray eggs marked with black spots are laid. The female alone incubates them for the necessary 13 to 16 days. Young leave the nest some 14 to 18 days after hatching.

Rough-legged Hawk

With strong migratory drive. the Rough-legged Hawk winters throughout the plains states and nests all across the Arctic from Alaska to Newfoundland.

It gets its name from its fully feathered legs and feet. and although this feature is hard to see at a distance. it is not too difficult to distinguish from other large hawks.

Because its feet are relatively small and weak. it preys on mice. lemmings. and other small prey. It thus hunts close to the ground much like the smaller Marsh Hawk or Harrier. Few other large hawks regularly hunt in this manner.

The Rough-legged Hawk *(Buteo lagopus)* is 19 to 24 inches (48.3 to 61 cm) long and has a wingspread of 48 to 56 inches (121.9 to 142.2 cm). It has two color phases. In the dark phase the body is all brown except for some white that shows at the base of the primary feathers when seen from below. In the light phase the back and wings are brown. but the underparts are white. When seen from below. the wings and tail are white with clearly marked dark borders at the trailing edges. There is also a dark patch at the bend of each wing.

The bird shows little fear of man. and is frequently killed by cars when feeding on traffic-killed animals. And although all hawks are protected by federal law. unwary Rough-legs are shot by hunters more than other members of the Hawk or *Accipitridae* family.

It usually hovers. flaps. and glides close to the ground. but the Rough-legged Hawk sometimes flies to great heights. becoming no more than a speck to the ground observer.

In March. flocks can be seen moving north. By April very few birds remain in the winter range. Silent fliers. the birds become vocal only during the mating season when they cry so shrilly that Eskimos call them Squalling Hawks.

The birds use a variety of nest sites. ranging from the open tundra. to rocky crags. or trees. Pairs will often have several nests and use a different one each season. Built of willow sticks and material from other northern plants. the nests are 24 to 30 inches (61 to 76.2 cm) in diameter.

The egg season and the number of eggs depends on the supply of food. particularly lemmings. If they are plentiful. the egg-laying season will be from April to June with five to seven eggs being laid. If the lemmings are scarce. just two or three eggs may be laid as late as July.

Usually incubated by the female. the eggs hatch after 28 to 31 days. Young leave the nest about 41 days after they hatch.

Return flights to the prairie begin in September and may continue through October.

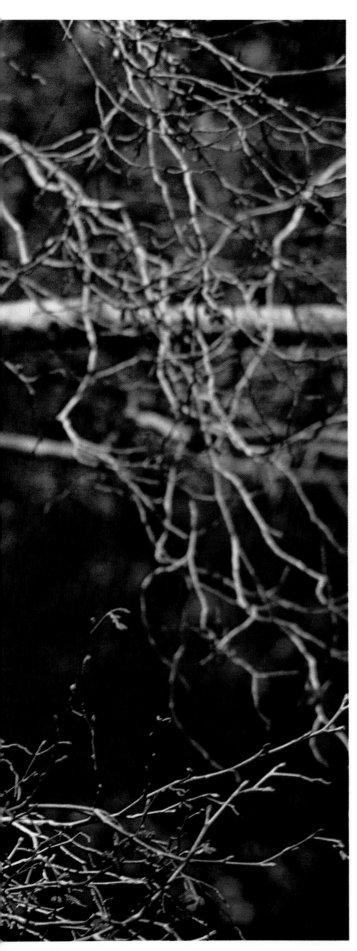

EASTERN WOODLANDS

Few regions of the world are as rich and varied in vegetation as the Eastern Woodlands of North America. In the Great Smokey Mountains of North Carolina and Tennessee there are more species of trees than in all Europe.

The bird life is no less rich, nor varied. From the soaring Bald Eagle to the darting Ruby-throated Hummingbird, the birds of the region represent almost every bird family found in North America.

In pioneer days the deciduous forests stretched in a solid mass from the Atlantic Coast to the boundaries of the prairie well west of the Mississippi River. Although virgin trees have been cleared, and today's forests are made up of second growth, enough woodland remains to attract a unique community of birds. And as of old, it is a community ruled by the seasons.

In no other region of the continent are the seasons so clearly defined. The many deciduous trees, stark in the winter, lush in the spring and summer, and aflame with yellows and reds in the fall allow no uncertainty about the time of the year. And the annual influx of great flocks of migratory birds accent spring with both song and visual delight that no one can ignore.

Many of these migrants have tropical origins and retain strong ties with the South American jungles. The hummingbirds and the tanagers, for example, are ambassadors for large families of birds. Most of them, however, never wander far from the equator. New World orioles, on the other hand, are migrating members of a rather stationary family which includes the blackbirds and meadowlarks that are found in great numbers in North America.

The turkey, which also had tropical origins, winters in North America with no apparent inclination to join the flocks of migrants. Some of these migrants, like the swallows, have Old World ties, but as a general rule, the birds with origins or at least relatives in the Old World lack a strong migratory urge.

While the Belted Kingfisher, Whip-poor-will, Blue Jay and Loggerhead Shrike may retreat before winter snows, few of them leave North America entirely.

American Robin'

No other bird of the continent is as well known and as much looked for as the American Robin. Even those benighted souls who ignore birds are usually able to recognize this one.

Although the American Robin *(Turdus migratorius)* is well distributed from coast to coast, it is more conspicuous in the eastern states through its winter absence. Northern

Left: The familiar American Robin is easily spotted over most of North America in the warm weather.

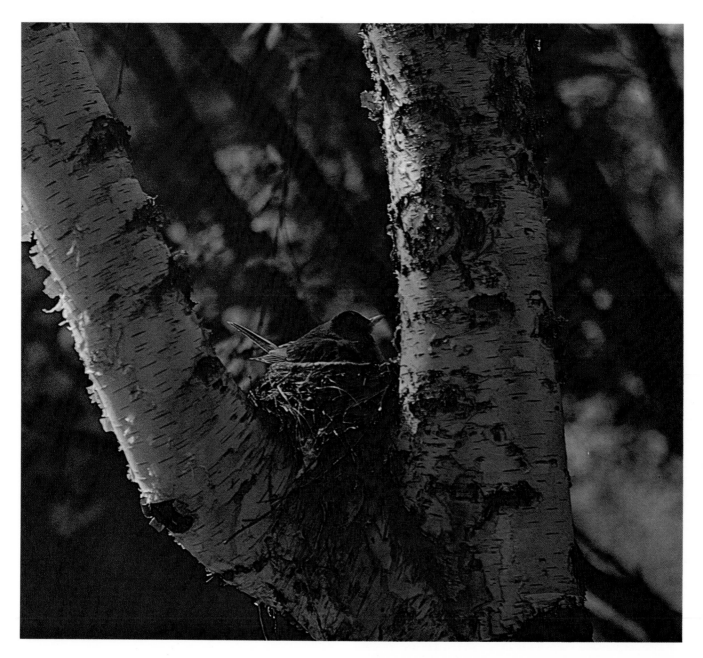

movement follows spring warming with strict fidelity. When minimums fall below 37°F (2.8°C) the robin is not found. When minimums rise above that point, however, the robin appears.

Migration from the winter range in the southern states, Mexico and Guatemala begins in February. By March, most males have arrived in the northern states and early in April, as soon as the females arrive the male begins singing their familiar *cheer-cheer-cheer-up.*

In many of the western states migratory movement is less predictable, but east of the Rockies the American Robin is a true harbinger of Spring. Wisconsin, Michigan and Connecticut have each adopted it as their state bird.

Although it is also called Redbreast and Robin Redbreast, the American Robin and the Robin Redbreast of Europe are not the same species. The latter, though also a member of the Thrush or *Turidae* Family, is a smaller bird more closely related to American bluebirds.

The American Robin is 9 to 11 inches (22.9 to 27.9 cm) long. In breeding plumage, the male is mostly gray above with dark head, wings and tail. Outer tail feathers are white tipped. The breast is light brown to dark, earthy red. Females have paler markings, and the breasts of the young are speckled with white.

Although there are 306 members of the Thrush family in the world, just 19 of them are found in North America. Most of these are noted for their clear, liquid song and their lack of fear.

In rural areas robins are most frequently seen in fields at the edge of forests or other dense cover. In urban areas they can be found in parks and gardens, often on lawns.

When feeding, their habit of running a few steps and then stopping with cocked head makes it seem as if they are listening for worms and grubs beneath the ground. Recent studies, however, have made it fairly certain that the bird hunts by sight rather than sound.

Opposite: A Robin incubates in her nest high in a tree where, in summer, branches keep the air cool. In early spring the nest is hidden in dense bushes or branches for extra insulation from cold air.
Above: Juvenile robins lack the red breast of adults.

Robins that have just pulled a fresh worm from the ground are sometimes mugged by other, thieving birds. The English Sparrow *(Passer domesticus)* is particularly adept at the grab and run game. Robbins also eat grass-hoppers, caterpillars, ants and several types of fruits and berries.

Nests, neatly cupped of grass and mud, are usually built well up in trees or artificial structures, but some birds may nest on the ground. Eggs of well-known 'Robin's egg blue' are laid from April through June. There are usually four eggs and incubation, almost entirely by the female, takes from 12 days to two weeks. Young can fly when 14 to 16

days old. Except for the most northern migrants that build their nests at the limit of the boreal forests, Robins usually raise two broods a season.

Scarlet Tanager

Tanagers make up a large family of New World birds that are only scantily represented in North America. Most of the 236 species of these colorful perching birds live in tropical South America. Just four species fly north to breed, nest and raise their young each summer.

The migrants, however, make up in brilliant plumage what might be lacking in numbers. The Hepatic Tanager *(Piranga flava)* of the southwest is maroon red, and the Summer Tanager *(Piranga rubra)* which ranges from coast to coast is rose red. The Western Tanager *(Piranga ludoviciana)* of the western mountains, has a red head, yellow body, and black wings, while the Scarlet Tanager *(Piranga*

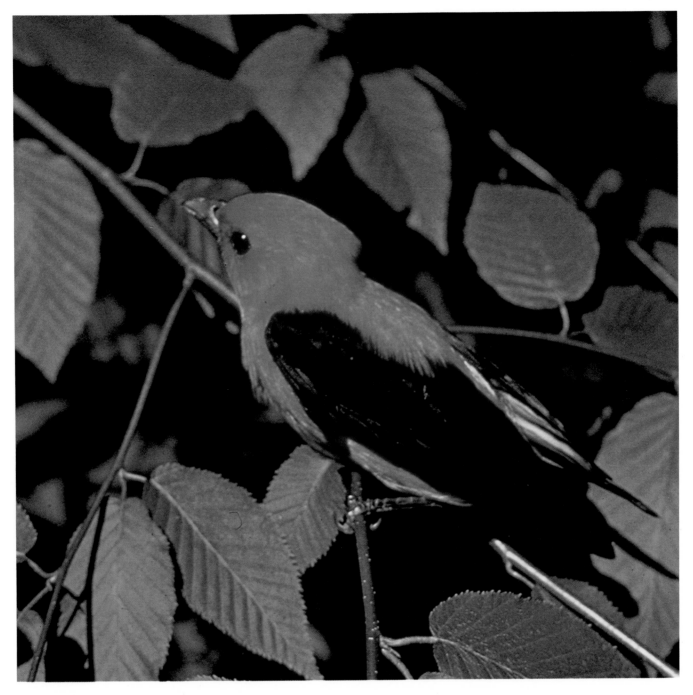

olivacea) of the eastern woodlands has black tail and wings and a bright red body.

Actually, only the males have the bright dress, and often it fades soon after the breeding season. Females and males in fall and winter are usually dull green or pale yellow.

Tanagers eat a great variety of insects, many of which are harmful to trees and crops. They also eat slugs, snails, worms, fruit and berries. The birds can best be attracted to feeders with breadcrumbs of a mixture of peanut butter and cornmeal.

The Scarlet Tanager is 6½ to 7½ inches (16.5 to 19 cm) long. In winter, both male and female are dull green above and pale yellow below. In early spring, with their plumage changed to bright red and black, the males lead the migration from South America. They arrive in the United States

Opposite: It is from high perches that the male American Robin breaks out in cheery song.

Above: The Scarlet Tanager male will lose this vivid coloring when the breeding season draws to a close.

through April and appear in southern Canada by mid-May.

Nesting trees are usually deciduous hardwoods such as oaks, hickories and ash. Females arrive several days after males. Birds have a caroling song with a burr that is best phrased by *queer, queery, queerit.*

When courting, the male hops among low branches flashing his bright back to the female who watches from a higher branch. The nest, built by the female, usually well out on a high limb, is a saucer of rough twigs, pine needles,

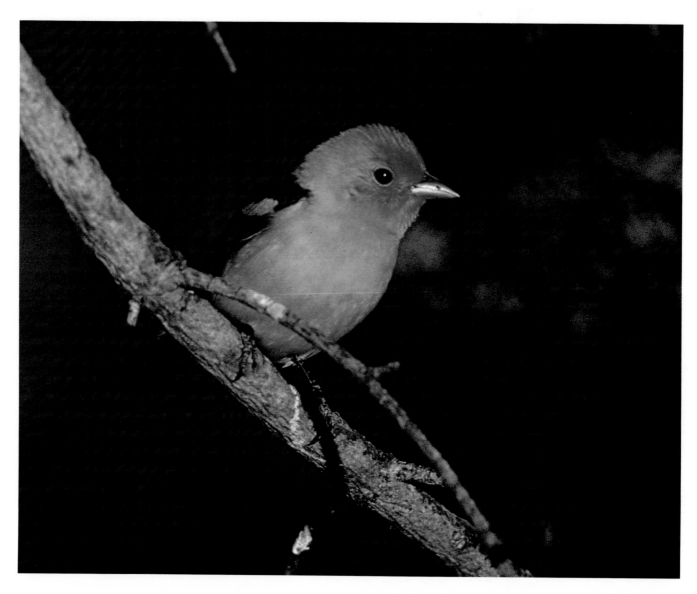

Above: The singing voice of the Western Tanager is vigorous but harsher than the American Robin's.
Opposite: The Blue Jay is unobtrusively protective of its nest, yet it is also a noisy and bold bird.

and grass. Four pale blue eggs with brown spots are laid during the nesting season which begins in May in lower latitudes and extends to August farther north.

Incubation by the female takes 13 to 14 days, and the young leave the nest 9 to 15 days after hatching. More than any of the other North American tanagers, the Scarlet Tanager is a frequent host to the nest-parasite cowbird.

Baltimore (Northern) Oriole

The males of both the Baltimore and Bullock's subspecies have bright orange bodies with black tails, backs and wings. The Bullock's has a single wide wing bar of white, while the Baltimore has a single, narrow wing bar. The head and throat of the Baltimore is entirely black, while the Bullock's has an orange throat and orange streak above the eye. Female of the Bullock's Oriole is olive

green above and buff white below. It has two white wing bars. The female Baltimore is similar except it is yellow instead of buff white below. Birds are 7 to 8 inches (17.8 to 20.3 cm) long.

The Baltimore Oriole was reportedly named for Sir George Calvert, first Baron of Baltimore and one of the early colonizers of Maryland. As the story goes, the lord chose a livery of orange and black, a combination that gave his name to the bird.

The other Northern Oriole subspecies was named for William Bullock, who was one of the first to collect a specimen of the bird for his museum in London.

Behavior of the subspecies varies only slightly to adjust for differences in habitat. Both Bullock's and Baltimore females weave hanging, bag-like nests some six inches (15.2 cm) deep. Both usually lay four eggs which they incubate for about 14 days. After another 14 days, the chicks are ready to fly.

Northern Orioles are insect eaters and strip trees of many damaging insects such as aphids, weevils, leaf-eating caterpillars and wood boring larvae, but they also eat fruit which puts them out of favor with orchard owners.

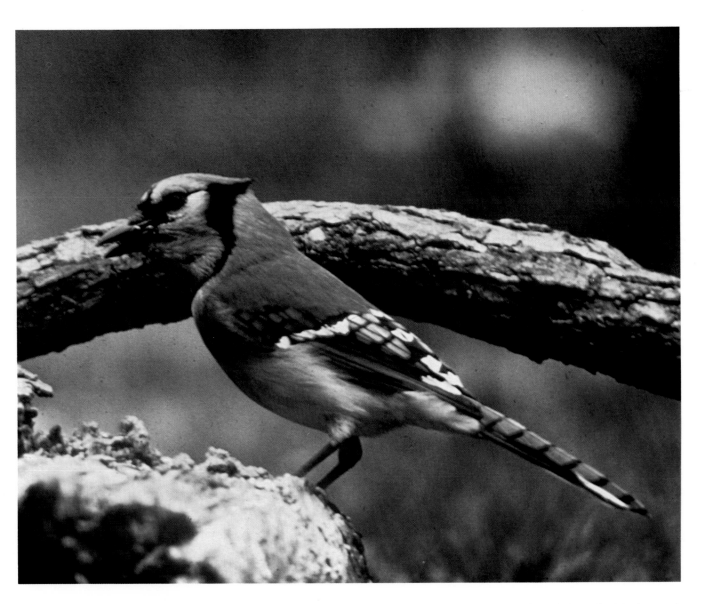

The birds come to feeders, and will take a variety of offerings, including peanut butter and sections of orange. They have also been known to sip from hummingbird feeders. Because of feeding by humans in the eastern states and Canada, more and more Baltimore Orioles are staying north in the winter. The bulk of the birds, however, still fly south in the fall to Mexico and South America.

Not only is the Baltimore Oriole not a true oriole, but by recent reclassification, it is also not even a distant species. It is one of two subspecies of the Northern Oriole *(Icterus galbula)*, the other being the Bullock's Oriole.

The Bullock's Orioles' summer range extends from the Pacific Coast well into the plains states. Baltimore Orioles are found from the Atlantic to the Plains States. Even though the birds have slightly different markings, where their ranges overlap they will interbreed freely. Discovery of their interbreeding was good cause for reclassification of these birds.

New World Orioles not related to orioles of the Old World are members of the Troupial Family which includes the blackbirds, grackles and meadowlarks. Most of the Troupials winter in or close to their nesting area, but the orioles with strong migratory drive winter in Mexico and South America.

Blue Jay

While the Scrub Jay *(Aphelocoma coerulescens)* and the Steller's Jay *(Cyanocitta stelleri)* inhabit the western deserts and mountains, the Blue Jay's domain begins east of the Rocky Mountains where it becomes the most prominent representative of the Crow or *Corvidae* family.

Like all members of the family, the Blue Jay *(Cyanocitta cristata)* is noted for its intelligence. Crows, jays, magpies, and nutcrackers have an extensive 'vocabulary' of calls which they use to communicate with their own kind and perhaps with other species.

Although pairs are usually solitary during the nesting season, Blue Jays have a highly developed social sense. Pairs' bonds are strong, and old birds are often cared for. In several cases, blind birds have been fed and led to water by other jays.

Perhaps the most remarkable thing about the Blue Jay, however, is its vocal talent. It cannot only imitate many other birds, but its range of utterances runs from softly whistled melodies to raucous jeering.

By imitating a hawk's shriek, the jay can make other birds dash for cover. The high call of *jae-jae* is most often heard when the bird finds an enemy such as an owl or a cat in its territory. Other common calls include a fast clucking and a two-syllable, ringing call that suggests a bell tone.

The bird, 11 to 12½ inches (27.9 to 31.8 cm) long, is white below with a blue back, tail, and crest. Its white face is bordered with black, and its wing and tail feathers are patterned with blue, black and white. Plumage for male and female is alike.

Blue Jays eat almost anything. Curious about all things, they are particularly curious about food. Generally, they eat three times more vegetable matter such as seeds, nuts and berries, than animal matter such as insects, fishes, frogs, mice, small birds and bird eggs. They can easily be attracted to bird feeders, but often they chase smaller birds away.

Blue Jays that nest in the Canadian north move south for the winter, but many birds stay year round in their nesting range. Nesting season, governed by the climate, runs from March to August. The first step for most pairs is the construction of a false nest, a loose platform of twigs. It is followed soon by the true nest usually about 10 to 15 feet (3 to 4.5 m) up in a tree or bush. Built of twigs, lichens, moss and grass, it is 7 to 8 inches (17.9 to 30.3 cm) in diameter.

Four to five pale blue to pale green eggs, spotted with brown or gray, are laid. Incubation, often entirely by the female, takes about 17 days. The bird can fly 17 to 21 days after hatching.

The birds, also known as Blue Coats, Common Jays and Jay Birds, defend their nests by diving at, pecking at and screeching at any intruder, including man.

Loggerhead Shrike

While the Shrike Family is a large one with 74 species, most of them live in the Old World. Just two species, the Loggerhead Shrike, unique to the New World, and the Northern Shrike (known as the Grey Shrike in Great Britain) are found in North America.

Shrikes are the only predatory songbirds, and like other predators, they have keen eyesight. A Northern Shrike can recognize a mouse from 240 feet (73 m), and spot its own kind from 1,250 feet (381 m).

Although shrikes prefer insects which they can take on the fly and swallow in one gulp, they also kill small rodents and birds. Shrikes can often be seen perched on a limb or other high vantage point waiting for prey.

A shrike can take a smaller bird in flight by catching it in its strong feet or by striking it on the ground with its hooked bill. Shrikes often store prey, particularly rodents

Right: The only western jay to have a crest, the Steller's Jay inhabits the forests where it likes nesting in the conifers.

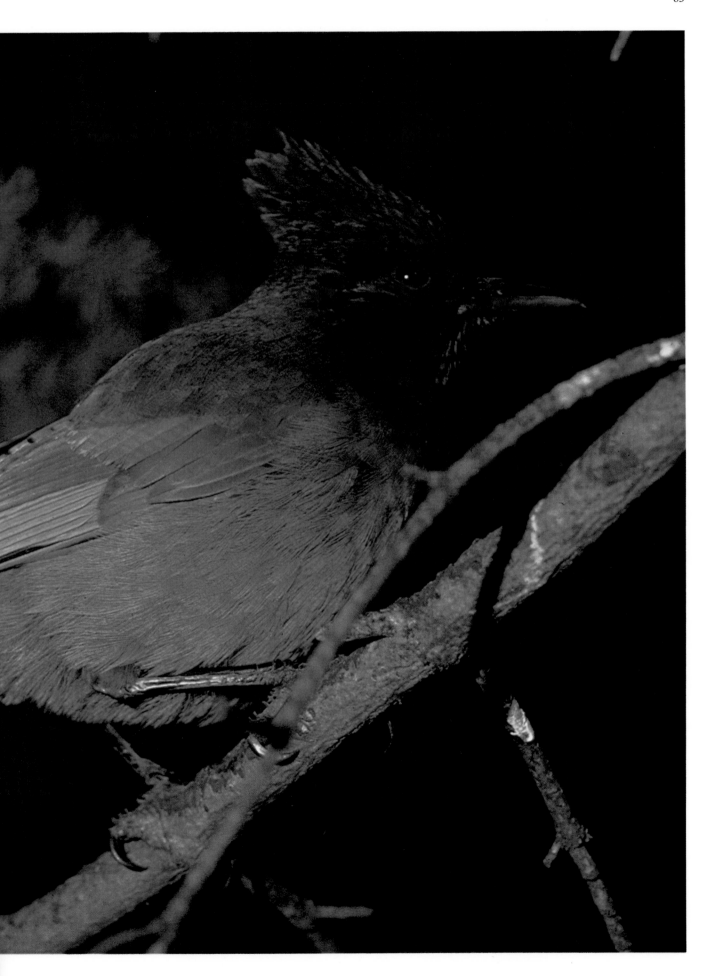

and birds, by impaling them on a thorn or the barbs of a wire fence. The stored food is usually eaten eventually. Shrikes do not appear to be wanton killers.

The Loggerhead Shrike is eight to ten inches (20.3 to 25.4 cm) long, slightly smaller than the Northern Shrike. Both birds are gray above and white below with black wings and tails, patterned with some white. And both have black, mask-like bands running toward the eyes. The Loggerhead's mask, however, meets over the bill. The Northern Shrike's does not. Females of both species have similar but duller markings.

Both species migrate, but the Northern Shrike's summer nesting range extends into the Arctic. The Loggerhead Shrike is rarely seen north of central Canada.

In the southern portion of the Loggerhead's range, nesting can begin as early as February. Both parents build a cup-shaped nest of twigs and grass in a bush or tree. They line the nest with hair, feathers, or string. After four to seven dull white eggs with buff spots are laid, probably both birds or possibly just the female take on incubation duties. Chicks hatch in about 16 days and leave the nest some 20 days after hatching.

Although shrikes can sing melodically, they are best known for their harsh rattling and rasping cries. The Loggerhead's larder is sometimes raided by mockingbirds, but smaller robbers are kept away both from hunting and nesting territory by the shrike's aggressive fluttering.

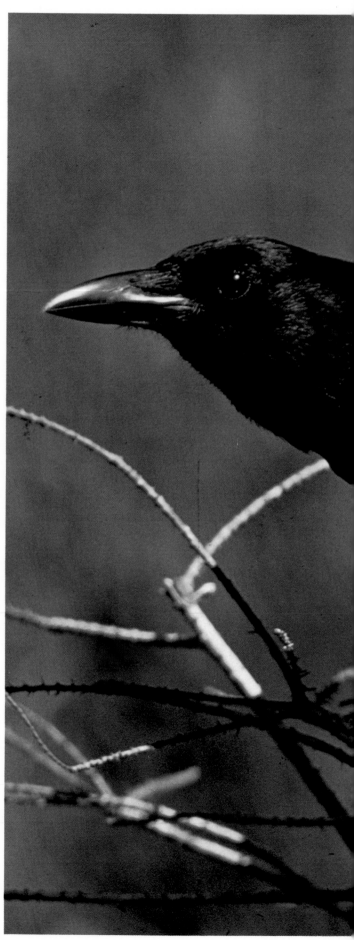

Above: Loggerhead Shrikes live in open areas where there are high perches from which to pursue prey.
Right: The Common Crow (*Corvus brachyrhynchos*), known for plundering nests, also alerts animals to danger.

Ruby-throated Hummingbird

Hummingbirds. which are all natives of South America. are among the world's most unusual birds. Not only can individuals perform surprising aerial stunts, but the Hummingbird or *Trochlidae* Family has evolved with astonishing diversity.

At latest reckoning there were 319 species ranging from the Cuban Bee Hummingbird just 2¼ inches (5.7 cm) long to the Giant Hummingbird 8½ inches (21.6 cm) long. Beaks of the many different species have evolved with specific shape and size to draw nectar from specific blooms. The profusion of blooms in the equatorial jungles may explain in part the diversity of the family.

Many species have evolved, however, to survive in regions outside their native jungle. Hummers are found in the high Andes as well as the Amazon Valley. And a few birds have adopted migration patterns that take them across large bodies of water all the way to North America.

Some of these migrants appear only rarely in Southern Florida or along the Mexican border. but there are eight species that nest regularly in the United States and Canada. Of these, the Ruby-throated Hummingbird *(Archilochus colubris)* is the only one that nests east of the Mississippi.

The male Ruby-throat is green above and white below. Its gorget of iridescent feathers appears black in the shade but it flashes with fiery red in the sunlight. The male bird also has a slightly forked tail. The female, also green above and white below, has no gorget. Its throat is white, and the female's tail is not forked.

Adult birds are 3 to 3¾ inches (7.6 to 9.2 cm) long and have wingspreads of 4 to 4¾ inches (10.2 to 12.1 cm). In addition to the hum of their wings, Ruby-throats squeak out a rabid call which will give away their presence even when they cannot be seen.

In light of their small size, the travel of the migrating hummingbirds are astounding. Starting in Central America, some Ruby-throats do not stop to nest until they reach Canada. The Black-chinned *(Archilochus alexandri)* and the Calliope *(Stellula calliope)* Hummingbirds, both western nesters, also extend their range into Canada, but the Rufous Hummingbird *(Selasphorus rufus)* takes the prize for high latitudes. It makes an annual trip from Mexico to its nesting range in Alaska and the Canadian Arctic. Other migrants nesting west of the Mississippi are the Costa's *(Calypte costae),* Allen's *(Selasphorus sasin),* and Broad-tailed *(Selasphorus platycercus)* Hummingbirds.

Opposite: A Rufous Hummingbird feeds from a foxglove. Even if replete, these birds defend their food source.
Below: A female Rufous. When feeding she will fend off encroachers with her distinctive tail movements.
Overleaf: Increased use of feeders has helped guarantee a constant food source for the Anna's Hummingbird.
Page 90/91: A Rufous Hummingbird perches.

Only the Anna's Hummingbird *(Calypte anna)*, found in its California nesting range year-round, seems to have lost the migratory drive.

Like the other migrating hummingbirds, the Ruby-throat times its travels to take advantage of the peak bloom of nectar-bearing flowers. Usually flying singly with males preceding females, the birds arrive in the southern states in March and early April. They are not seen in Canada until mid-May.

A busy feeder, the Ruby-throat, with wings whirring, goes from flower to flower almost too quickly for the eye to follow. It can fly backward, forward, sideways, straight up or down, and it can hover. Its wings are a blur of motion. High speed movie cameras used to time wing beats for the Ruby-throat show that it uses 55 strokes a second to hover, 61 strokes when backing, and 75 when flying forward.

The male's courtship flight, which may also be used to defend territory, takes it back and forth in swooping arcs as if it were swinging on a pendulum. The high hum of the wings on these flights becomes a whistle. Like many other hummers, Ruby-throats probably copulate in the air.

The nest, built of spider webs, thistledown, lichens, and other delicate plant growth is just 1 to 1¼ inch (2.5 to 3.2 cm) in diameter, but it is big enough to hold the two, tiny eggs. Incubation takes 16 days, and it is 20 to 22 days before the young can fly.

Below and right: The smallest North American hummingbird is the Calliope (female below). When performing a courtship display or defending his food source, the male will rise impressively and sweep down to buzz his mate or foe.

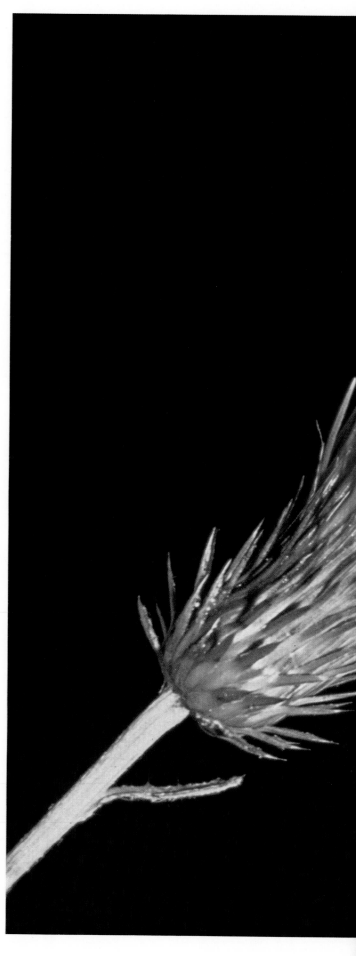

Because of the high metabolism, hummingbirds must feed almost constantly to maintain their supply of fuel, but they are able to slow their heartbeats at night to save energy in a kind of hibernation. They also have the ability to store fuel. Before leaving Florida and Georgia each fall to cross the Caribbean, Ruby-throats feed heavily to add layers of fat under their skin. They do not take flight until they have increased body weight some 50 percent.

Turkey

Since the days of Benjamin Franklin, the first person of note to suggest it, the turkey has been a candidate to replace the Bald Eagle as the national bird of the United States.

Certainly, the recent encouraging comeback of the Wild Turkey speaks well for its endurance, and this American native apparently played an important role in history. If the many stories can be believed, the turkey *(Meleagris gallopavo)* saved many early settlers from starvation, and perhaps even kept some of the colonies themselves going through lean times.

Domestication of the Turkey with selective breeding that led to an unusually heavy-bodied fowl, was begun by the Indians, particularly in Mexico, and it was a Mexican subspecies that the conquistadors took to Europe in the Sixteenth Century. English settlers brought the domesticated bird back to the New World.

The Wild Turkey, however, did not fare well, especially in the eastern states where it was almost wiped out by heavy hunting. In the early 1900s it looked as if the Wild Turkey was headed for extinction, but careful management of important breeding grounds combined with planting of new flocks has helped the bird make a gradual comeback. By 1970, an estimate based on counts in thirty states put the Wild Turkey population at 1,250,000.

The present range of native and introduced flocks spreads from the Eastern Seaboard all the way west into parts of California, Oregon, and Washington. The bird has even been successfully transplanted to Hawaii.

Controlled hunting has reestablished a tradition for hundreds of sportsmen. The Wild Turkey is an attractive quarry. The largest of upland game birds in North America, it is 36 to 48 inches (91.4 to 121.9 cm) long and has a wingspread of 4 to 5 feet (121.9 to 152.4 cm). Males are generally larger, perhaps 10 inches (25.4 cm) longer than females.

The patterned shades of brown plumage glow with iridescence varying from metallic bronze, gold, and red to green. Wings are brown barred with white while the back and tail are brown barred with black. When held erect the

Opposite: A female Costa's Hummingbird feeds her young. Costa's eat nectar, insects and red flowers.
Below: Destruction of the Wild Turkey's natural habitat has compounded the problem of decreasing numbers.

square-tipped tail feathers form a fan. Males strut with puffed chests and fanned tails during their splendid courtship display.

Turkeys like thick cover of low brush or trees for night roosting. They prefer to feed in early morning or late afternoon, browsing fields, meadows and forests for seeds, nuts, acorns, certain fruits and grains. They will also eat insects and small reptiles.

In the breeding season, males strut and gobble in a clearing to attract the females. Usually just the oldest, strongest gobblers mate. Breeding can begin as early as February in warm climates and as late as mid-June in colder areas. Actually, males gobble in any season, and both birds have a variety of clucks and low squawks for warning or calling others in the flock. Flock sizes vary from 25 to as many as 500 birds.

Nests are shallow scrapes, big enough to hold some 10 to 12 eggs. Incubation by the female alone takes 27 or 28 days, and chicks are usually ready to follow the adult bird from the nest a day after hatching. In two weeks, the young chicks can fly a few feet and reach low perches.

Cliff Swallow

The swallows that faithfully return to their nesting nooks at California's Mission San Juan Capistrano each spring are carrying on a tradition that began in 1776, the year the mission was established.

The bird, one of eleven members of the swallow family found in North America, is a Cliff Swallow *(Petrochelidon pyrrhonota)*, and its nesting range extends from coast to coast and from central Mexico into the subarctic regions of Alaska and Canada.

It is thus a mistake to think of Cliff Swallows exclusively as California or even west coast birds. They might be found anywhere that there are eaves or wall niches to give foundation for their mud-daub nests.

It is also a mistake to credit the birds with a precise schedule. Contrary to the myth, they do not appear at the Capistrano mission on St Joseph's Day (16 March) every year. Like all swallows, the Cliff Swallow's northern progress is governed by the hatch of flying insects. If the hatch is early due to a warm spring, the swallows might reach their nesting sites two weeks before their arrival date of the previous year.

Swallows and the larger martins make up the Swallow or *Hirundinidae* Family. North America has four martins and seven varieties of swallow, just a small portion of the 79 known members of the family. Although flight patterns and other traits are similar to swifts, swifts and swallows are not related. In fact, swallows have no close relatives.

The Cliff Swallow, 5 to 6 inches (12.7 to 15.2 cm) long, has a back, crown and tail of very dark blue that appears black in shadow. Its rump is rusty brown, its throat and face, reddish brown, and its sides gray-brown to gray-green. The belly is white and there is a white patch on its forehead. While many other martins and swallows have deeply forked tails, the Cliff Swallow's tail is almost square. The tail helps avoid confusion with the Barn Swallow *(Hirundo rustica)* which shares the same nesting range.

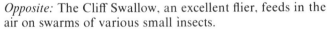

Opposite: The Cliff Swallow, an excellent flier, feeds in the air on swarms of various small insects.

Above, both: A Violet-green Swallow *(Tachycineta thalassina)* feeds her young. These social birds live and nest in colonies, partly for protection.

Because buildings provide the overhangs that swallows prefer for their nests, the birds have benefited from human settlement, at least in rural areas. It is believed that the swallows were once limited to natural caves and were able to expand their nesting range only as human settlement spread.

There are some puzzles in this story. Cliff Swallows and Purple Martins *(Progne subis)*, abundant in some areas, are not seen in other areas that seem similar in every way. One explanation might be that prolonged rains in some past season may have forced flocks to abandon certain areas changing traditional flight patterns. Another cause may be the practice of certain home owners to destroy nests because of drippings or noise.

All members of the swallow family are long-distance migrants. The Cliff Swallow, like the others, winters in South America, but it does not fly as far south as the Barn Swallow which sojourns in Argentina 7,000 miles away.

Cliff Swallows nest in colonies. Their nests, made of mud balls built up with surprising speed by both birds, are shaped like round bottles with either a short neck or simply a hole for an entrance. With continuous daylight flights

from the mud source to the nest, a busy pair can complete its nest in five days.

Although trees and cliffs are sometimes used, eaves of barns or homes seem to be preferred. Some colonies number more than a thousand birds.

Egg season, governed by the climate of the area, runs from April to August. Four or five cream to pink eggs, sometimes spotted with brown, are laid. Incubation by both birds take 12 to 14 days, young can fly in about 16 days.

Belted Kingfisher

One of the most refreshing sounds my hiking partner and I ever heard was the happy chatter of a Belted Kingfisher. It came after a long, thirsty hike, and it told us that there was fresh water ahead.

The Belted Kingfisher *(Megaceryle alcyon)*, which ranges from coast to coast and as far north as Alaska and the Canadian Arctic, is by far the most common of the three North American kingfishers. The other two, the Green Kingfisher *(Chloroceryle americana)* and the Ringed Kingfisher *(Megaceryle torquata)* are seen only casually in some of the southern states.

Never far from the seacoast or fresh water streams or lakes, the Belted Kingfisher is one of the fishing kingfishers, distinguishing it from many Old World members of the family that do not fish. The Belted Kingfisher dives

from its high perch and often plunges well below the surface to come up with a small fish wriggling crosswise in its sharp beak. If the prey is close to the surface, the bird can scoop it up without breaking its flight.

Often the Belted Kingfisher, after returning to a favored perch, will beat the fish on a twig before tossing it in the air and gulping it down.

The bird has a blue-gray head, back, wings and tail and a white collar and white belly. The 'belt' is a band of blue-gray separating the collar from the belly. Mature females have an additional belt of chestnut across the belly and rufous sides.

The birds have a ragged double crest which combined with the long bill makes their heads look too big for their bodies. They are 11 to 14½ inches (27.9 to 36.8 cm) long.

In addition to fish, kingfishers also eat tadpoles, frogs, crabs, snakes, turtles, and even mice. They also catch flying insects on the wing. Undigested material is disgorged as pellets which serve to line the kingfishers' nest.

The nest itself, excavated in the side of a mudbank, might be at the end of a tunnel 3 to 7 feet (91.4 to 213.3 cm) long. It takes from three days to three weeks to build, depending on the hardness of the soil, but old nests are often re-used, saving the birds heavy mining work with their beaks.

From six to seven eggs can be laid any time from April to July. Incubation takes 23 or 24 days, and young birds can probably fly early in their fourth week.

Above: A Belted Kingfisher shows off its colorful plumage and the crest on its large head.
Opposite: Perched on the forest floor, a Whip-poor-will displays its excellent natural camouflage.

Except for those that venture into the Arctic in the summer, most Belted Kingfishers winter in their nesting range. They usually fish alone, but when birds do come together, there can be a great racket and much playful chasing up and down the course of a stream or along the coast of a lake or bay.

Whip-poor-will

A bird that is heard far more than it is seen, the Whip-poor-will gets its name from its tireless call that is sometimes written "RIP-purple" but more often rendered "WHIP-poor-will."

Fifty to 100 repetitions of the call are common, but the naturalist John Burroughs (1837-1921) once counted a record 1,088 consecutive calls. The bird is most often heard from dusk until about 9:30 p.m. and from about 2 a.m. until dawn.

A night feeder on insects which it catches on the fly, the Whip-poor-will *(Caprimulgus vociferus)* roosts on the ground or on a limb by day. Like most other members of the Nightjar or *Caprimulgidae* Family, the Whip-poor-will perches lengthwise on limbs or fences.

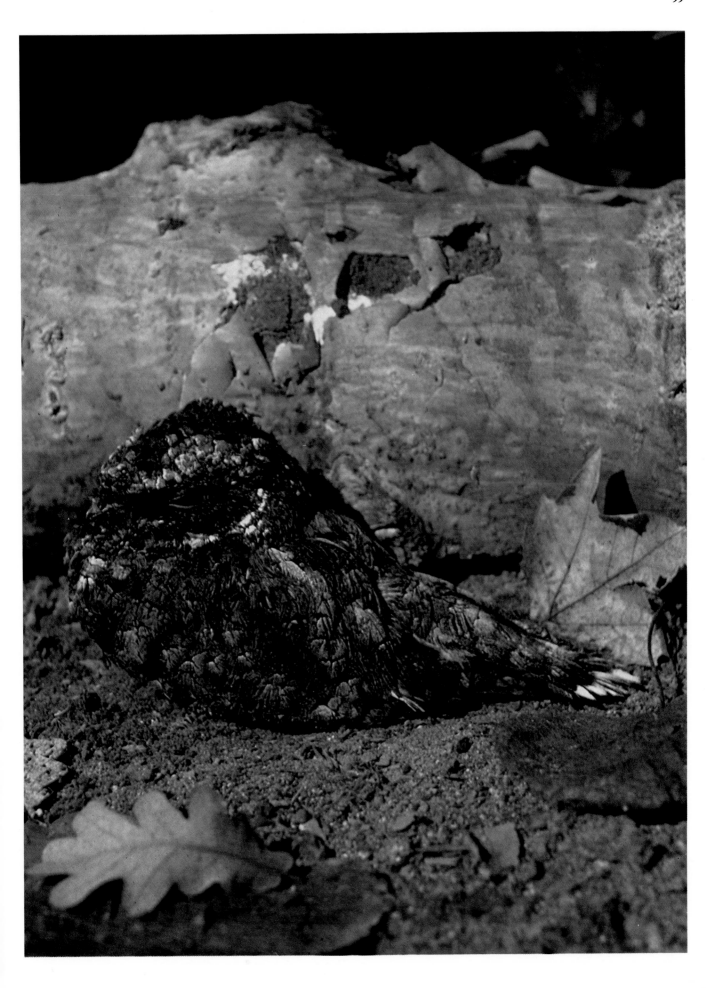

The mottled Common Nighthawk blends perfectly with its woodland environment. It is usually seen flying at dusk, although it does fly during the day.

One of seven Nightjars found in North America, it is common in spring and summer months throughout the eastern states. Its nesting area extends into Nova Scotia and Central Canada and westward across the Southwest to Southern California. In the fall the birds retreat to the southern border and gulf coast states. Some even fly to islands of the Caribbean.

The bird, 9 to 10 inches (22.9 to 25.4 cm) long, is mottled brown, but males show white patches on their tails when they fly. If flushed from its daytime perch, the bird gives the impression of a large moth in silent flight.

One of the Whip-poor-will's favorite habitats is a wood-lot with plenty of undergrowth. Here its protective coloring makes it almost impossible to see no matter if it is perched on the ground or among the tangled branches of shrubs or trees.

Eggs, usually just two, can be laid as early as May or as late as August, depending on the latitude. They are laid on the ground without any preliminary nest building. Incubation, probably by the female only, takes 19 or 20 days, and it is another 20 days before young birds are able to fly.

Whip-poor-wills enjoy a good dust bath, and because the finest dust for bathing is often found along rural road-sides, they are often caught in the headlights of automobiles. The bird's eyes show red in the glare.

Nightjars are closely related to owls, and the Whip-poor-will with its silent flight and restless night call, is particularly owl-like. Other North American Nightjars include the Common Nighthawk *(Chordeiles minor)*, Chuck-will's widow *(Caprimulgus carolinensis)*, Buff-collared Nightjar *(Caprimulgus ridgwayi)* and Poor-will *(Phalaenoptilus nuttallii)*.

Bald Eagle

Because it is a scavenger and a thief, the Bald Eagle's standing as a national bird has often been challenged. It isn't even unique to North America. The Bald Eagle's range extends into northeast Siberia, and some individuals have wandered as far off as Sweden.

Nationalism aside, however, it must be said that the Bald Eagle *(Haliaeetus leucocephalus)* is a magnificent flier, arrestingly handsome, and big enough to command respect. Body length varies from 34 to 43 inches (86.4 to 109.2 cm) and wingspread from 6 to 7.5 feet (182.9 to 228.6 cm).

Adults of both sexes have the same markings, a white head and tail, and a brown to black body. The eyes, unfeathered legs and feet, and large, hooked beak are yellow. Plumage of immature birds is dark brown. The head does not turn white until the birds are four or five years old.

Eagles are unusually large hawks and thus belong to a family that has 208 species world-wide. Some 50 of these

Right and overleaf: The stately Bald Eagle can be found where there is a good supply of fish. Chemical contamination of its food has contributed to the declining numbers of Bald Eagles outside Canada and Alaska.

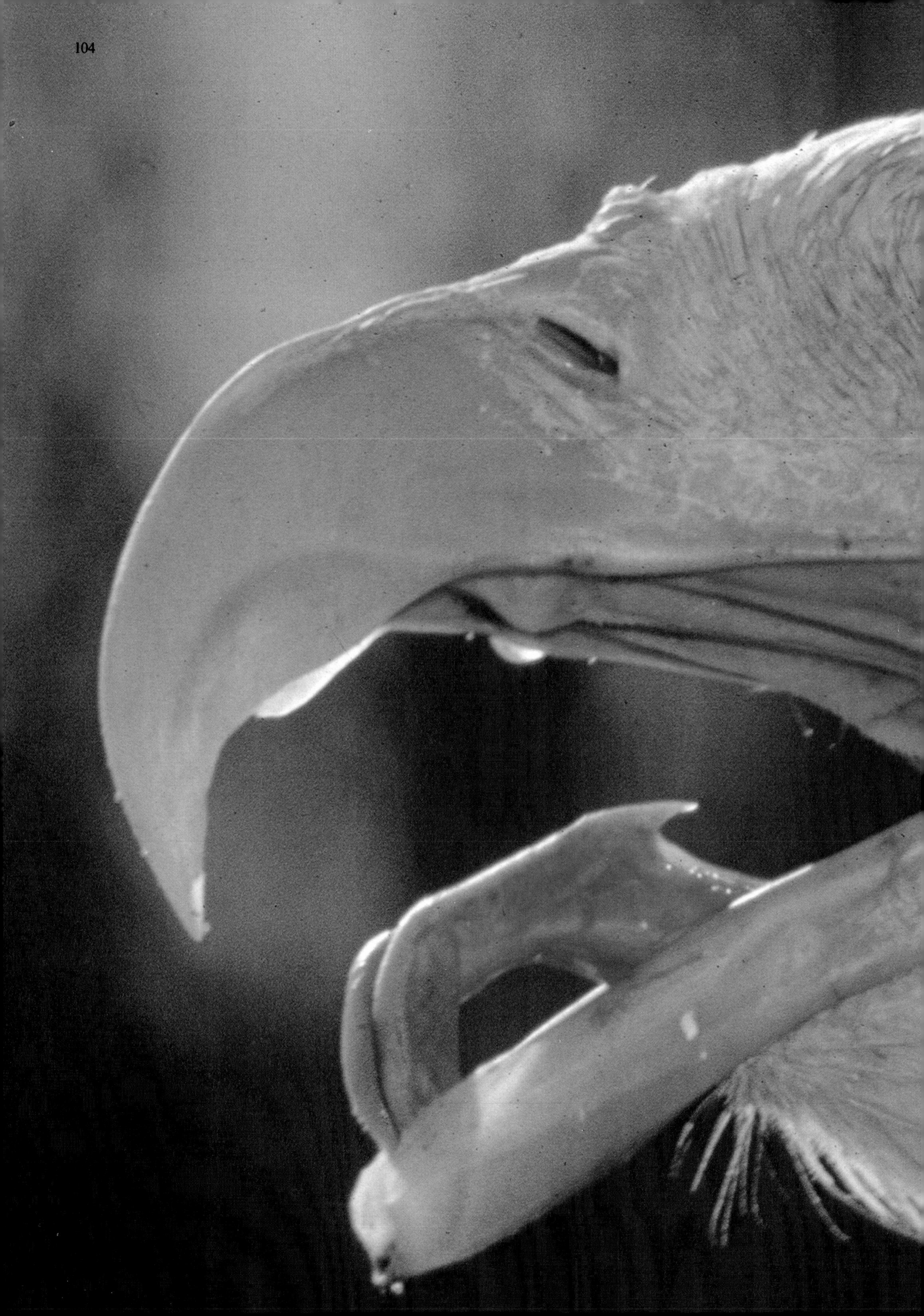

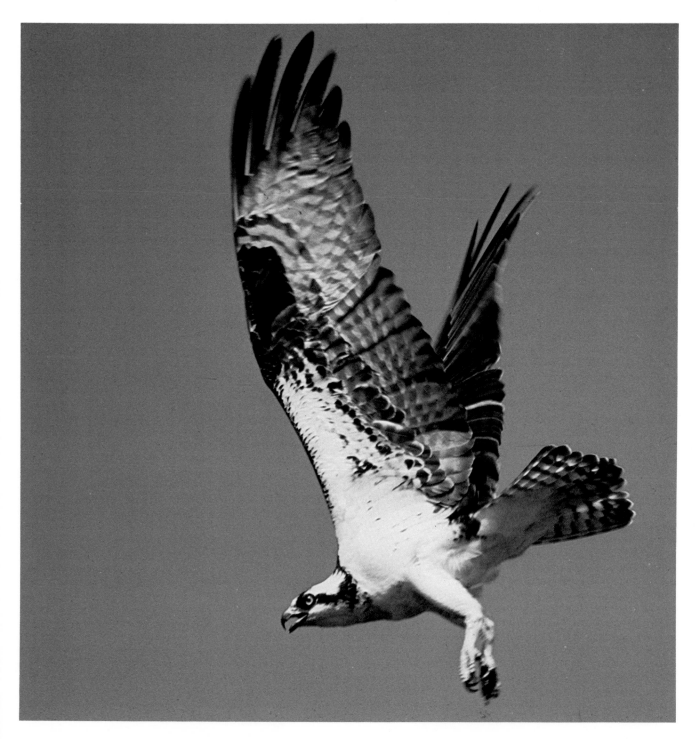

Opposite: The Golden Eagle is common in the West where it feeds on rodents in the canyons and rangelands.
Above: The Osprey, which feeds entirely on fish, hovers before plunging for food. This species is found worldwide.

have been classified as eagles. North America has just four eagles, and two of them, the Steller's Sea Eagle *(Haliaeetus pelagicus)* and the White-Tailed Sea Eagle *(Haliaeetus albicilla)* are probably Old World birds that have extended their range to North America. The other bird, the cosmopolitan Golden Eagle *(Aquila chrysaetus)*, is also seen in Asia, Africa and Europe.

The Golden Eagle is not closely related to the Bald Eagle. The latter has a larger head and beak and unfeathered lower legs. A sea eagle, it is a fish eater and rarely strays far from water. The Golden Eagle hunts for land animals, and is often seen over mountains and inland plains.

The Bald Eagle's soaring skills almost match those of the Turkey Vulture. In fact, at a distance, the two species can be mistaken for each other. The eagle, however, soars with wings flat while the vulture usually keeps its wings in a slight uplift.

Bald Eagles often fly in pairs, and when food is plentiful, they will gather in large numbers. The biggest concentration occurs in Alaska during the salmon run. From

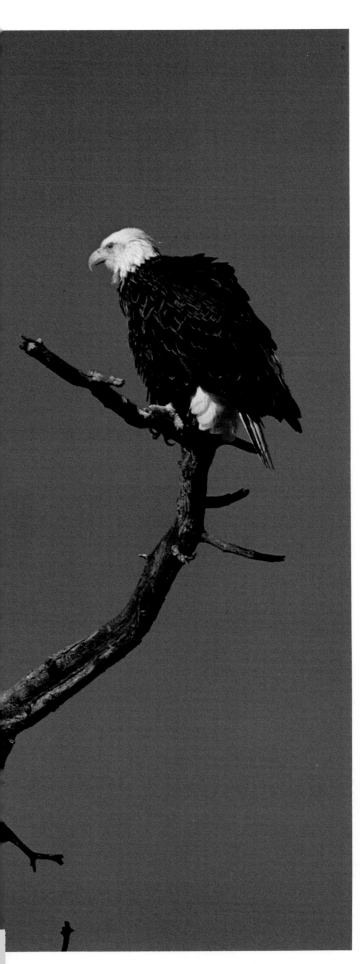

3,000 to 4,000 Bald Eagles have been counted feeding on weak or dead salmon in a ten mile (16 km) stretch of Alaska's Chilkat River.

Outside of Alaska, however, the population of Bald Eagles has been declining steadily. Even though they are protected by law, birds are frequently shot. Human disturbance of nests, loss of nesting trees and pollution of water also account for the decline.

Several years ago, when both Bald Eagles and Ospreys were more plentiful, it was a common sight to see aerial piracy above the fishing grounds. The hawk-like Osprey *(Pandion haliaetus)* evolved enough differences, particularly in its strong talons, to be classed in its own family apart from the hawks. It dives for fish and pulls them from the water with its talons.

If there is a Bald Eagle hovering above, it will swoop down on the Osprey and harry it until it drops the fish. The Osprey may try to get above the eagle, but the eagle is a stronger flier and is not weighed down with a fish.

When forced to drop the fish, the Osprey gives a loud and angry screech. The eagle dives and catches the prize, usually well before it hits the ground.

Bald Eagles also catch fish on their own, and they prey on muskrats, squirrels, rabbits and other mammals. Eagles will take ducks, but usually only those that have been wounded by hunters. Bald Eagles also include carrion in their diet and sometimes vie with vultures for traffic-killed animals along roadsides.

The Bald Eagle takes top honors for the biggest nest for a single pair of birds. The mass of sticks with lining of moss, pine, needles or grass, may be as much as eight feet (243.8 cm) wide and 12 feet (365.7 cm) deep. It is usually built in a tall tree, but some pairs build nests on rocky crags.

Usually two dull white eggs are laid. In Florida and other warm areas, the egg laying season runs from November to January. Farther north, laying may not occur until early May. Incubation is believed to take about 35 days. Soon after hatching, rivalry between chicks begins. If one chick is weak, the stronger will eventually kill it. Birds fly some 75 days after hatching.

Left and above: Adult and juvenile Bald Eagles rest in the tamarack trees of Montana, one of the stages of their journey southward. They nest in the tall trees.

COASTS AND WATERWAYS

Hospitable habitats for waterbirds are not limited to continental shores. The smallest inland pond will attract ducks. In fact, most ducks prefer nesting areas with fresh water.

Below: Snowy Egrets over the Russian River in California. Like other herons, the sexes are identical in appearance, and consequently they perform the same roles in courtship and in nesting.

Gulls range far inland and big flocks of them populate the Great Lakes and Utah's Great Salt Lake. Gulls are often seen following a farmer's plow many miles from the nearest water. Great Blue Herons, though most often seen feeding in shallow water, will also range into meadows where no open water can be found.

It must also be remembered that the majority of water birds are long distance migrants, and their routes along the Atlantic, Mississippi, Central, or Pacific flyways often take them far from water. But, of course, the long flights lead to a watery habitat for summer breeding or winter survival.

Waterbirds include many superlative species. The Trumpeter Swan is the largest of all swans. The Canadian Goose is perhaps the most majestic water fowl and the Pelican the most unusual. The Flamingo is considered by many the most handsome.

The Wood Duck, however, is a strong rival for the beauty prize. And hosts of other water birds, though more common and less colorful than the Wood Duck, are just as vital in their environments. Ponds and sheltered bays would lose part of their character without winter flocks of Canvasback Ducks. And without the Surf Scoter or the Willet the seashore would be a strangely different place.

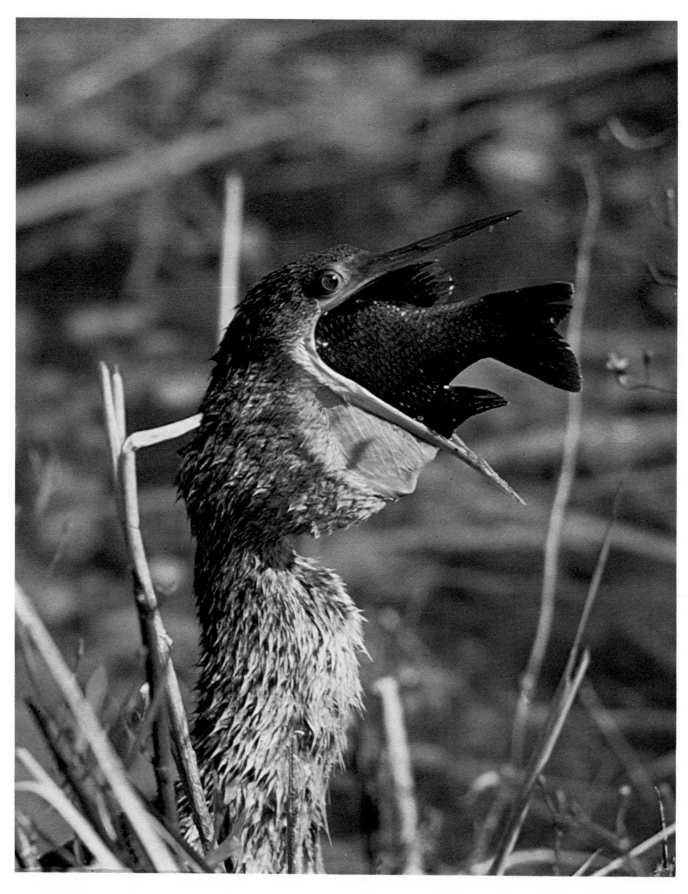

Above and opposite: The Anhinga (*Anhinga anhinga*) is common to the tropical swamps of Florida, but breeds irregularly. Here it spreads its wings to dry.

Overleaf: The Common Murre (*Uria aalge*) lives in the open sea and returns to cliff tops or rocky ledges, where it gathers in large colonies for breeding.

The all-black Pelagic Cormorant (*Phalacrocorax pelagicus*) is the smallest cormorant of the Pacific coast. It nests with colonies of other cormorants on the narrow ledges along the faces of coastal cliffs.

Herring Gull

Of all North American gulls, the Herring Gull *(Larus argentatus)* is most widely distributed. It winters on both the Atlantic and Pacific coasts and in many regions of the interior where there is water.

Also common in Europe during the winter, most Herring Gulls nest in the Arctic or subarctic. Some nesting colonies, however, remain in Wisconsin, Minnesota, Michigan and Ohio. Along the Atlantic Coast, gulls have nested as far south as North Carolina.

Although gulls are often difficult to identify, the adult Herring Gull combines black wingtips with flesh-colored legs. The California Gull *(Larus californicus)*, also a large gull with black wingtips, has green to green-gray legs.

The Ring-billed Gull *(Larus delawarensis)* is smaller but its markings are similar to the Herring Gull's. The Ring-bill, however, has a black band near the tip of both mandibles. The Herring Gull has a red dot on the lower mandible only.

Though not as large as the Great Black-backed Gull *(Larus marinus)*, the largest of the North American species with a wingspread of 5 to 5½ feet (152.4 to 167.6 cm), the Herring Gull is still impressive. It is 22 to 25 inches (55.9 to 66 cm) long, and has a wingpread of about 4½ feet (137.2 cm).

The adult bird is white with a gray mantle and black wingtips. Except for the wingtips, it is all white from below. The bill and eyes are yellow.

Like all gulls, young birds go through several molts to progress from dark brown to the contrasting black, white, and gray of adults.

Top and opposite: Herring Gulls live in the tundra and along coasts where there are cliffs or islets for nesting. In winter it moves to the coastal areas.
Above: The Heermann's Gull (*Larus heermanni*), foreground, can often be found trailing fishing boats.

In flight, Herring Gulls often move in flocks that circle as they rise. In normal weather the bird flaps slowly and glides expertly to take advantage of headwinds and updrafts. When excited, the bird is quite vocal with cries of *clew-clew-clew* or *caak-caak-caak*.

There are few things a gull will not eat. It scavenges in harbors for garbage, follows the farmer's tractor for grubs and worms, patrols the coast for crustaceans or fish that might have washed up on a shore and takes a good share of live fish. It does not dive like the terns and some of the smaller gulls, but lands on the water to scoop up prey in its beak.

Both: Smaller than the Herring Gull, the California Gull is found inland. This species is known for having saved the Mormon's first crop from a locust infestation.

Like most members of the Gull or *Laridae* Family which includes kittiwakes, noddies, and terns, the Herring Gull has strong social instincts and nests in colonies, usually on bare ground. The nests are little more than hollows rimmed with grass or seaweed.

Egg laying, depending on climate, runs from May to August. Usually three spotted eggs ranging from blue to brown are laid. Incubation takes 25 to 27 days and young begin flying after about 42 days.

Parents feed their young by regurgitation. The food at first is held in the beak for the chick to grab. After chicks are a few days old, however, the adult simply regurgitates onto the ground near the nest where the chicks can peck the food up.

Chicks have a high, whistling screech which seems to be interrupted only for a feeding.

Also known as the Common Gull, Harbor Gull and Winter Gull, the Herring Gull has remarkable longevity. Two birds in captivity lived to 45 and 49 years respectively. A banded bird that lived in the wild was 31 years old when it died. Perhaps other gulls live as long, but so far few of them have been studied as thoroughly as the Herring Gull.

Top: These gulls have just hatched, after nearly a month of incubation.

Above and opposite: The Herring Gull is less common in the West than on the East Coast, where it has survived in greater numbers by learning to scavenge extra sources of food from dumps and fish canneries.

Overleaf: This Ring-billed Gull feeds on earthworms, plentiful in fields and meadows after rain.

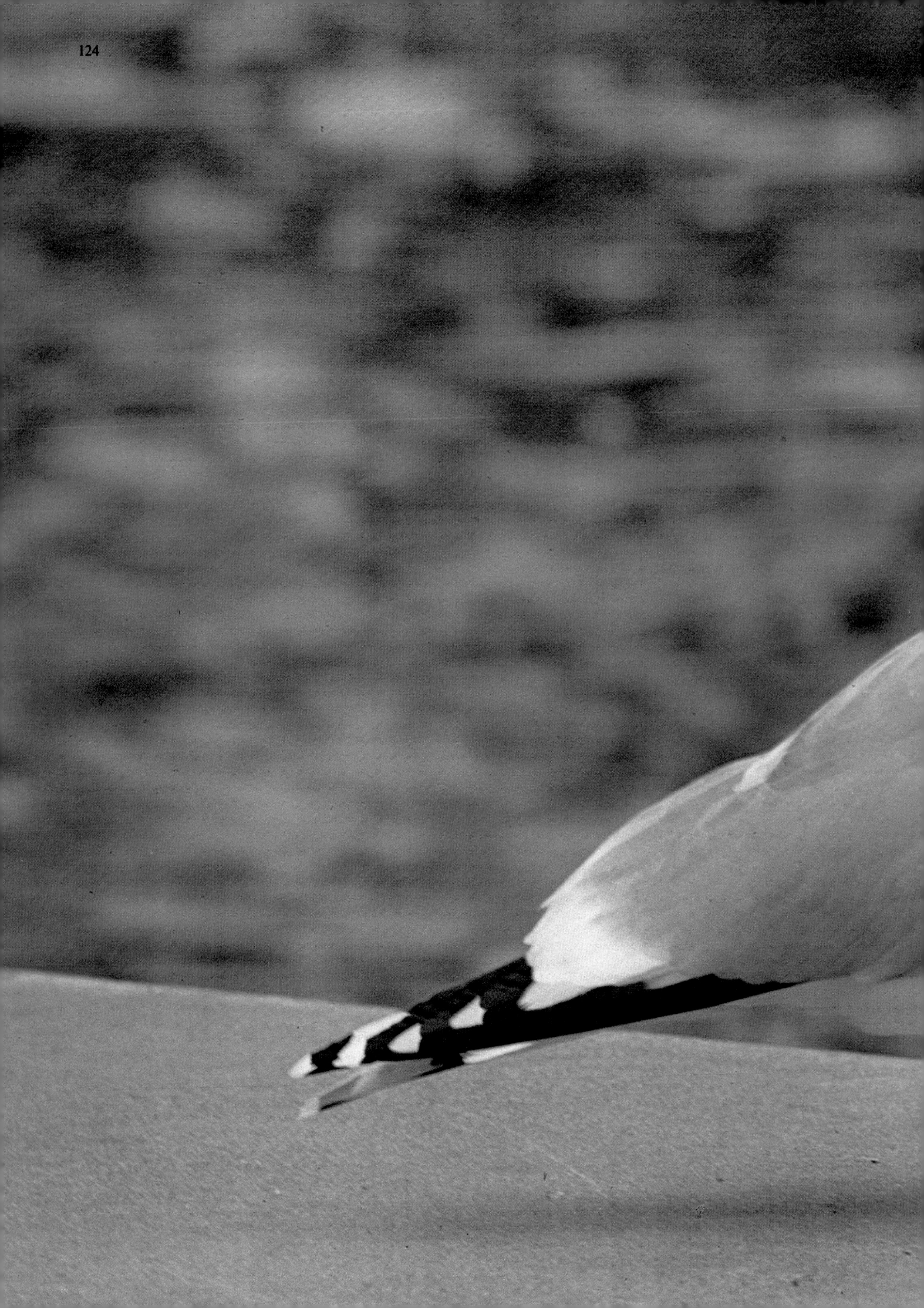

Great Blue Heron

Although the Great Blue Heron *(Ardea herodias)* is claimed as an American native, it is so similar to the Old World's widely distributed Grey Heron *(Ardea cinerea)* that the claim is suspect. The two birds may well be subspecies with a common origin.

It is certain that the Great Blue, and the Great White Heron, which is a subspecies, are the biggest North American representatives of the family *Ardeidae.* The family includes bitterns and egrets as well as herons. There are 63 species of *Ardeidae* world-wide, with 15 in North America.

Great blues stand four feet (121.9 cm) high and have wingspreads up to seven feet (213.4 cm). Males are slightly larger than females. With long dark legs, sharply pointed beaks, and long necks, Great Blues, like all herons, fly with legs extended and necks folded. Cranes, on the other hand, fly with both legs and necks extended.

Except for some white around the head and on the neck, plumage of Great Blue Herons varies from light gray to slate blue. Some birds show a cinnamon tint on the neck.

Well equipped for wading, the birds are usually seen near the edges of lakes, rivers, bays, or oceans. But they also frequent swampy land and sometimes venture far inland to hunt on fields and meadows.

Their main food is fish, amphibians and crustaceans, but they will also eat insects, rodents and birds. They can spear large prey with their beaks, but usually they grab food between the mandibles. When hunting, they walk slowly with only slight motion of the head and neck. When they spot a fish, frog or other prey, they strike with a snake-like thrust.

Above and left: In a typical pose, a Great Blue Heron stands at the water's edge, where it dwells among the dense reeds and trees. These birds are known to venture considerable distances for food when it is scarce nearby.

Top: The Sandhill Crane (*Grus canadensis*) is seen less often outside the Arctic owing to a diminishing habitat.
Above: Unlike other large, white herons, the Great Egret has a yellow bill and black legs and feet.
Opposite top: This young Wood Stork (*Mycteria americana*) soars gracefully through the Everglades in Florida.
Opposite bottom: The Great Egret once faced extinction because of the demand for its snowy white feathers.

Although solitary hunters, Great Blue Herons usually nest in colonies often with closely related species such as Great Egrets *(Casmerodius albus)* and Snowy Egrets *(Egretta thula).* New nests are often a platform of sticks some 18 inches (45.7 cm) across built high in a tall tree, but because pairs return to the same nest and add to it year after year, it might grow eventually to a massive structure four feet (121.9 cm) in diameter.

Pale olive to blue-green eggs, usually four of them, are laid in early spring. Incubation by both birds takes from 25 to 29 days and during this period the birds will roll the eggs about once every two hours. Both adults feed the chicks by regurgitating food. Young begin flying about 60 days after hatching, but it may be 30 more days before they abandon the nest entirely.

The Great Blues' nesting range extends throughout North America and they retreat only slightly from the Arctic regions of Canada and Alaska during the winter months. Generally shy of man, the Great Blue utters a raucous squawk when startled, which explains why it is sometimes called Big Cranky. Wounded birds have been known to stab and severely wound people who have tried to pick them up.

The Great White Heron *(Ardea occidentalis)* occupies a restricted range in southern Florida where it freely

crossbreeds with Great Blue Herons. Great White populations are sometimes decimated by hurricanes. About 40 percent of the total population was killed during Hurricane Donna in 1960, but it took just three years for the colony to recover. Aerial counts have since set the population at some 1,500 birds.

Trumpeter Swan

The hero of a conservation success story, the Trumpeter Swan *(Olor buccinator)* is the largest swan in the world and the largest waterbird in North America.

Sexes are similar with all white plumage, black legs and feet and black bill, but males are bigger than females. An adult male might be six feet (182.9 cm) long and have a wing-spread of 8 feet, two inches (248.9 cm).

The Trumpeter Swan lacks the orange spot at the base of the bill which is an identifying feature of the Whistling Swan *(Olor columbianus).* Instead, Trumpeters have a 'grin line', a flesh-colored stripe at the base of the bill.

Probably the best identifying feature, however, is the loud and deep cry of the Trumpeter. Best described phonetically as *ko-ho,* the cry sounds much like the horn of an ancient automobile. The cry is most often heard when the bird is in flight.

In shallow water, Trumpeters feed on the leaves and stems of plants simply by submerging their head and neck, but in deep water they tip up like a duck to reach their favorite food. They can also use their feet to dig up roots and other growth from the bottom of lakes or ponds.

Early settlers in Canada and the United States found large populations of Trumpeter Swans. The bird bred from Alaska to Hudson Bay, south across the Great Plains, down the Mississippi Valley to the Gulf Coast, and west to the Pacific.

The bird, however, was slaughtered without restraint. Hunters not only shot down adults from the sky but also

Previous page: The Little Blue Heron *(Florida caerulea)* can be found in the Everglades but it breeds irregularly.
Left: Best known for its eerie call, the American Bittern *(Botaurus lentiginosus)* lives among the reeds.
Above: A family of Trumpeter Swans.

raided nests for the swan chicks or cygnets and the eggs. Swan pelts, in demand for millinery, powder puffs, and down coverlets, were collected by the thousands. From 1853 to 1877 the Hudson's Bay Company alone sold 17,671 swan skins.

By the turn of the century, Trumpeter Swans numbered fewer than 100 birds. Strict conservation efforts began in the 1930s with small colonies that had survived in the vicinity of Wyoming's Yellowstone National Park and Montana's Red Rock Lakes National Wildlife Refuge. Under protection, populations slowly increased, allowing government workers to reintroduce breeding pairs in other refuges. By 1968 there were 4,000 to 5,000 birds in the United States and Canada, and the population, still growing, is even bigger today.

The new generation of Trumpeters do not have a strong migratory urge. Except for some winter retreat from the extreme north, most birds stay in their nesting territory year-round, congregating wherever there is open, unfrozen water. Their nesting territory now extends from southeast Alaska into western Canada and south into Oregon, Nevada, Wyoming and South Dakota.

When the nesting season begins in late April or early May, the birds build a mound of reeds and grasses that may be five feet (152.4 cm) across. It is hollowed out to hold from four to six light cream eggs. Incubation, probably entirely by the female takes 32 or 33 days.

Young cygnets are vulnerable both to parasitic diseases and their careless parents who sometimes crush them. Al-

Top: Trumpeter Swans nesting. These snowy white birds sometimes build their nests on lodges that have been abandoned by beavers.
Above: This young Trumpeter Swan will not breed for nearly five years.

though survivors begin feeding with the adult birds soon after hatching, it takes some 100 days for them to reach flying age. Although swans begin to pair when they are three years old, they do not usually mate until they are five years old. The birds can afford some leisure because of their longevity. One captive bird lived for 29 years, and another for 32 years and six months, a ripe old age in the avian world.

Above: Snow Geese (*Chen caerulescens*) wintering in the Chesapeake Bay. In spring they will head for the Arctic tundra.
Left: Parent Canada Geese lead their young to feeding spots around the lake. Adults molt shortly after hatching and they are unable to fly for a time.
Below left: Canada Geese flock in a public park.

Canada Goose

Probably no other North American waterfowl is as well known as the Canada Goose, and perhaps no other bird is as difficult for the layman to identify precisely. The irony is due to a proliferation of subspecies.

There are at least eleven subspecies of Canada Geese, all with similar marking. Standard features of the bird *(Branta canadensis)* are a long neck, and black head with white cheek patches joined under the throat. The body is brownish gray with pale belly and black tail. The feet and bill are also black.

The difference among subspecies is size, varying from the 22-inch (55.9 cm) Cackling Canada Goose to the 48-inch (121.9 cm) long Giant Canada Goose. The latter has a wingspread of 75 inches (190.5 cm). Another difference is voice. The smaller subspecies have a high-pitched chatter while the bigger birds tend to utter musical honks of much lower tone.

All forms of Canada Geese migrate, flying both day and night, and usually taking V formation. They are often the first spring migrants. Some wintering in southern portions of the United States begin heading north in January. They move slowly, however, never advancing ahead of the thaw of lakes and streams.

Flocks are made up of family groups, geese being one of the few birds to retain family ties beyond the breeding season. Young fly south with their parents and remain with them through the northern migration. It is not until arrival at the Arctic breeding grounds that the parent birds will drive the yearlings away. And the yearlings move well away, sometimes more than 100 miles (160 km) from the breeding colony. They will not be ready to breed until they are two or three years old.

Geese return faithfully to the same breeding ground year after year and respect territorial barriers, which explains how the many subspecies arose and why they remain pure.

Contrary to popular belief, females, not the males in a flock, usually take turns at the lead during the long migrations. Because they fly both day and night geese take more advantage of landmarks than most other waterfowl that fly only at night.

Although most geese fly to specific breeding grounds in the Arctic and subarctic, a few colonies breed in the Rocky Mountains and isolated spots in the midwest. Nests are built of grass and sticks on elevated ground near water. In Arctic colonies, some four or five eggs are laid early in June. Incubation by the female under the male's guard takes 28 to 30 days. The young of small subspecies can fly in about 42 days. The larger subspecies cannot fly until they are at least 60 days old. All young, however, are able to leave the nest and follow their parents just 24 hours after hatching.

Above and top: Each year these Canada Geese and goslings will return to family breeding grounds. In the course of one migratory journey, the parents are able to teach their young the routes and ground locations.

Like many other members of the duck family, geese molt soon after their brood is hatched and lose their ability to fly for several weeks.

Flocks have a clear-cut pecking order. Pairs with families dominate mated pairs without families, while the latter dominate yearlings which in turn dominate immature birds. In the nesting colony, with much charging and hiss-

ing, the dominant birds will drive those with lesser status from their territory.

Canada Geese use all four North American flyways for their spring and fall migrations. Their winter range extends throughout southern Canada, the United States and into Mexico. But many of the subspecies have specific summer and wintering grounds.

The Aleutian Canada Goose, one of the smaller subspecies, for instance, is found only in the Aleutian Islands. The Cackling Canada Goose, a Pacific subspecies, breeds in Alaska and winters from California south into Mexico. Some individuals of this small goose have been seen in Japan and Hawaii.

The Atlantic Canada Goose, perhaps the best known of all the subspecies, ranges from Baffin Island, Newfoundland and Labrador south to Delaware. The Dusky Canada Goose breeds in Alaska and winters in a small area of Oregon's Willamette Valley. The Giant Canada Goose, once almost extinct, breeds in Manitoba and winters in Michigan, Minnesota and North Dakota.

Other subspecies are the Lesser Canada Goose, the Interior Canada Goose, Richardson's Canada Goose, Taverner's Canada Goose, Vancouver Canada Goose and Western Canada Goose.

Above: The White Pelican tends to be a quiet bird, occasionally grunting or groaning in low tones during the breeding season.

Pelicans

With its long beak and gular sac, heavy body and short legs, the pelican seems to be the most ill-proportioned bird imaginable. And, indeed, it is awkward on land where the dignity of its wobbling walk seems a studied pretense. In the air, however, pelicans are superb.

The Brown Pelican *(Pelecanus occidentalis)*, with white to yellow head and gray-brown body and wings, is 42 to 54 inches (106.7 to 137.3 cm) long with a wingspread ranging from 6.5 to 7.5 feet (198.1 to 228.6 cm). Yet it is much smaller than the White Pelican *(Pelecanus erythrorhynchos,* 50 to 70 inches (127 to 177.8 cm) long with a wingspread of 8 to 9.5 feet (234.8 to 289.6 cm). Browns weigh up to 8 pounds (3.6 kg), while Whites can weigh as much as 30 pounds (13.6 kg).

As members of the order *Pelecaniformes,* pelicans are related to cormorants, gannets, anhingas, frigatebirds and tropicbirds, all of which have gular sacs and feet with all toes joined by webbing (totipalmate).

By being able to spread the pliant bones of its lower mandible, the pelican can extend its gular sac into a large fish net. The bird scoops up a great deal of water when it takes a fish, but it lets the water drain from the sides of the beak before swallowing its prey.

White and Brown Pelicans live almost entirely on fish, and despite the size difference, both have the same awkward proportions. It is surprising therefore to note the many differences in behavior.

Brown Pelicans are divers, sometimes plunging from 70 feet (21.3 m) to hit the water beak first. The bird can continue several feet under water to catch its prey, but it usually bobs back to the surface quickly where it floats high on the water as it swallows the inevitable fish. White Pelicans, which also hunt their prey from aloft, glide to a feet-first landing on the water's surface where they scoop up the fish with a quick lunge with the beak.

Brown Pelicans are salt water birds and rarely venture inland while White Pelicans prefer fresh water lakes and are commonly seen inland. Both birds are social, but Brown Pelicans usually perch and hunt in small numbers. White Pelicans move in large flocks of about 25 to 100 birds, and when one bird flies, all fly. Both species fly in single file, but the Whites hold closer formation and are more likely to form Vs.

White Pelicans nest on islands and shores of inland lakes from southern Canada as far south as Texas. In winter, the flocks move south into a range extending from California and Florida down to Guatemala.

Brown Pelicans reverse the pattern. They fly south to spring nesting grounds extending from North Carolina and California down to South America. Few other North American migrants fly south to nest.

One notable exception is the Heermann's Gull *(Larus heermanni)*, a close associate of the Brown Pelican. This dark gull with bright orange to red beak will follow the pelican on its fishing sorties and usually manage to capture a dropped fish or fish fragment. Heermann's also fly south to nest and their breeding colonies are often next door to the pelican colonies.

Populations of both pelican species has declined in recent years due to chlorinated hydrocarbons and other agricultural pesticides which contaminate fish that the birds eat. The chemical causes thin shells which often make it impossible for the birds to raise young. Although the problem has not been studied extensively with Whites, they do not seem to be affected as severely as Browns.

American Flamingo

Once a regular visitor to the tropical swamps and shores of Florida, the shy American Flamingo *(Phoenicopterus ruber)* is now seldom seen in the wilds. Thus, in more ways than one, it is a rare sight.

Right: White Pelicans nest in colonies. Since their young are born without body covering, they must be protected from overexposure to the sun.

The bird is large and startlingly pink. Even the legs are pink. The primary flight feathers, however, are black, and the beak is white, tipped with black. The Flamingo's eyes are yellow.

It has developed unusually long legs and neck for feeding in shallow water. Even more specialized is the beak which is turned upside down when the bird lowers its head to feed. The beak bends sharply down at the middle. When feeding, the upper mandible dredges up mud. With rapid motions of the tongue, water is pumped in and out of the beak. Food such as algae, diatoms, small fishes, and crustaceans, are filtered by filaments that line the edges of the mandibles. When all mud is washed away, the bird lifts its head and swallows.

Flamingos fly and feed in flocks and need isolation. Although birds survive in captivity, wild flamingos fly at the first sight of man.

They use quick wingbeats with necks and tails extended, and flocks give the impression of a cluster of pink sticks soaring across the sky. They are rather long 'sticks'. Body length ranges from 36 to 50 inches (91.4 to 127 cm).

An evolutionary puzzle, flamingos were once thought to be most closely related to storks and ibises. Recent studies, however, suggest a closer relationship to geese and other members of the Duck family. Flamingos often sound like geese with their gabbling and deep honks.

Flamingos nest in the West Indies and South America where colonies of as many as 7,000 birds have been seen. The cone-like nests may be no more than two feet (61 cm) apart. Usually just one egg is laid, and it must be incubated for about a month. When the chick is about four days old, it is herded with other chicks in the colony into a

Above: Brown Pelicans fly in single file formation, flapping and gliding gracefully, low over the water.
Overleaf: The Wood Duck is frequently seen in parks.
Opposite: The Flamingo is a popular sight in the tropical tourist gardens of Florida, where it is protected.

group called a creche. After some 75 days, the young birds can fly.

American Flamingos are still seen casually from Texas to North Carolina, but the best chance for a look at wild birds is in Florida. In 1942, a flock of imported birds with clipped wings were released at Florida's Hialeah race track. They nested there for several years, raising about 65 chicks each season.

Also called Greater Flamingo, Scarlet Flamingo and West Indian Flamingo, the birds are relatively long-lived. One captive bird lived 18 years.

Wood Duck

If a beauty contest were to be held among the native birds of North America, the Wood Duck might well be favored to waddle off with the crown.

Many bird lovers contend that the Wood Duck *(Aix sponsa)* is the handsomest of all birds. If nothing else, the drake of the species certainly has a many-colored plumage that he wears with apparent pride.

The bird, 17 to 20 inches (43.2 to 50.8 cm) long, has a green head that shimmers with iridescent hues of gold and purple. Its red bill is bordered at the base with yellow and patterned on top with blue and white. A thin brow line of white arcs over the orange eye to join a straight line of ear

Above: The Purple Galinule (*Porphyrula martinica*) has large feet, enabling it to walk on lily pads.

Above right: Because they are sought after by hunters, Canvasbacks are being observed to protect their numbers.

Below: This male Ring-necked Duck (*Aythya collaris*) is a freshwater diving bird. In winter this breed disperses over the marshes to avoid attracting hunters.

feathers. The colorful head is further accented by a delicate white collar and chin strap.

The breast is chocolate brown or dark red flaked with white. The belly is white, the wings and tail dark, and the back dark touched with iridescence. The female has a grayish head with white rings around her brown eyes. Her throat is white and her breast and back are brown. The bill

is black. In his post-nuptial molt, the male looks much like the female except he keeps a brightly colored bill and has no white around his eyes.

Wood Ducks have short necks but hold their heads upright with bills pointing slightly down. They float high on the water with their short tails angled upward. When frightened, they take off almost vertically.

Not a deep diver but rather a dabbler, the Wood Duck is found in fresh water ponds and swamps in Pacific Coast states and in most states east of the Mississippi. It is rare in the Prairie and Rocky Mountain States.

Its nesting range extends to Prince Edward Island and Nova Scotia on the East and into British Columbia on the West. Apparently the smaller western flock remains apart from the larger eastern one. In winter, some birds migrate to Jamaica and Bermuda, but most remain in the continental United States, some as far north as Illinois and Maryland.

Wood Ducks seem better adapted to land than others in the duck family. They can walk easily and run swiftly. They nest in natural cavities in trees sometimes a mile (1.6 km) from water. In the non-breeding season, they raft in large numbers on ponds and marshes, but depart at dawn in small flocks.

They feed on aquatic plants, seeds, nuts and insects. One bird was killed with 65 acorns in its throat and crop. In the fall the ducks can sometimes be seen gleaning fields for corn or other seeds lost during harvest.

Early migrants, Wood Ducks arrive at the northern limit of their breeding grounds in March or April. Although pairs usually build their nest in the wilds, they have been known to select trees in gardens, parks and cemeteries. Some have even made the fatal mistake of nesting in chimneys.

Usually 10 to 12 white to dull brown eggs, much like chicken eggs, are laid. The female incubates them for the necessary 27 to 33 days. Soon after hatching, the chicks use their sharply-clawed feet to climb from the nest and down to the ground. The female calls from the ground until all the chicks have left the nest. She then leads the chicks to water where they begin to feed. Not returning to the nest again, the chicks learn to fly in about 63 days.

Other names include Bridal Duck, Acorn Duck, Swamp Duck and Tree Duck.

Canvasback Duck

One of the largest native American ducks, the Canvasback is a favorite of hunters and is consequently very shy, especially in the fall and winter hunting season months.

During migration, flocks in V formation fly high and fast. One bird was clocked at 75 miles (120.8 km) an hour.

The Canvasback (Aythya valisineria) is 19 to 24 inches (48.2 to 61 cm) long. Adult males weigh an average 2.76 pounds (1.25 kg) while adult females average 2.55 pounds (1.16 kg). Just one bird, needless to say, makes a healthy meal.

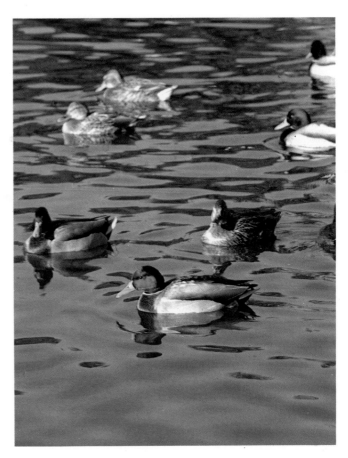

Above: The Mallard (*Anas platyrhynchos*) is the ancestor of the domestic duck. The male has a green head.
Overleaf: Female Blue-wing Teals (*Anas discors*).

The bird's name comes from the light gray back and white sides that are finely lined with dark to resemble the weave of canvas. The earthy red of the male's head and neck blends into a black breast to the waterline. The female has paler markings, but the red head is still evident.

The forehead of the Canvasback slopes, almost making a concave curve as it meets the curve of the beak.

Males are generally silent except during courtship when they croak, growl, and coo. Females are more vocal, quacking any time of year.

Diving ducks, Canvasbacks feed mostly on vegetable matter brought up from the bottoms of shallow bays or ponds, usually no more than 12 feet (3.66 m) deep. They are capable, however, of diving to 30 feet (9.14 m).

In addition to roots and stems, the duck also eats mollusks, fish and insects. It strains mud for seeds, and because of this, sometimes ingests spent birdshot which can cause death from lead poisoning.

Nesting sites near fresh water ponds and marshes extend from central Alaska, east to Manitoba, south to Minnesota and west into Northern California. In winter the birds retreat to warmer coastal regions near the Atlantic and Pacific where they are often seen on bays or at the mouth of rivers in large flocks. Some birds winter in Guatemala and Cuba, but most remain close to the North American mainland.

The Blue-winged Teal is named for the large blue area on its forewing, evident in flight. Teals are fast but cautious fliers and fly in small groups.

Slightly smaller than the Horned Grebe, the Eared Grebe (*Podiceps nigricollis*) breeds in colonies and all members raise their young at the same time.

Nests are built in thick clusters of water reeds, usually several yards or meters from open water. Made of sedges or bullrushes and lined with down, the nest is big enough for some nine or ten gray-green eggs which are laid from May to June depending on climate.

Incubation by the female takes 23 to 29 days. Chicks can swim with their parents soon after hatching, but young cannot fly for 63 to 77 days.

Other names for the Canvasback include White Duck, Bullneck, Can and Horse-neck.

Surf Scoter

Except for its bright orange bill and distinctive white markings on its head, the male Surf Scoter is a jet black bird, and it is one of the most common coastal ducks. It can be seen any winter day in or just beyond the breakers off Atlantic or Pacific shores.

A North American native, the Surf Scoter *(Melanitta perspicillata)* is a faithful migrant flying north in the spring to nesting grounds that extend from Alaska across northern Canada to Newfoundland.

The male, 17 to 21 inches (43.2 to 53.3 cm) long, has a white streak on the nape of his neck, a white patch on his

Opposite: Horned Grebes (*Podiceps auritus*) nest on floating, anchored nests in small groups or as a single breeding pair. They eat fish and tadpoles.
Below: The profile of these male and female Canvasbacks shows their distinctive sloping foreheads. In winter they remain out in the water, watchful of their enemies.

forehead, and a white crescent near the base of its orange bill. Females are dusty brown and lack the contrasting white patches, but they do have a pale white spot on either side of the head.

Like the other North American scoters, the White Wing *(Melanitta fusca)* and the Black Scoter *(Melanitta nigra)*, the Surf Scoter plays a daredevil game in breaking waves. As a breaker approaches, the bird waits until the final moment before diving to let the white turmoil pass over it. Then it bobs up immediately in the foamy wake of the wave to swim high on the surface until the next breaker comes. When not among the breaking waves, Surf Scoters' are usually found just beyond them, rising and falling on the incoming crests.

All scoters, however, will fequent sheltered waters of bays and marshes. They feed mostly on crustaceans, fish, sea worms, and other small marine animals, but they occasionally eat eel grass and other vegetable matter.

From the top of a cliff north of San Francisco early one spring I once observed four Surf Scoters, three males and one female, in a strange ritual. The males formed a triangle around the female who played a fickle game. She would select one male to swim beside. Then with much charging and splashing, the two would chase the other single males away. This continued until the female abruptly changed partners, joining'one of the other males to chase the two remaining away. This ritual, perhaps a preliminary phase of courtship, continued through the two hours I remained at my observation spot.

Surf Scoters nest near freshwater marshes or lakes, using a depression to build a cup of reeds beneath a concealing

shrub or tree. Seven or more buff to pink eggs are laid. Incubation period and age of flight of chicks is unknown.

By late September and early October, most birds have returned to their winter habitats along the coasts. Surf Scoters have many other, descriptive names including Skunk Head, Baldpate, Patch Head, Surfer and Surf Duck.

Although the males sometimes utter a low croak, Surf Scoters are generally silent, and unlike Black Scoters, their wings do not whistle loudly on take-off.

Willet

Although gray and nondescript when seen feeding along the shore of sea, lake or river, the Willet *(Catoptrophorus semipalmatus)* is the easiest member of the Sandpiper or *Scolopacidae* Family to identity.

All that is required is to see the bird fly. If startled, it rises with a loud, high-pitched cry of several syllables that end in *willet*. And the instant the bird spreads its wings it shows a surprising pattern of black and white. None of the other 51 representatives of the Sandpiper have such sharply contrasting wing patterns.

The family includes curlews, dowitchers, dunlins, godwits, knots, redshanks, snipes, the Ruff, the Sanderling, the Woodcock and of course, several sandpipers. They are generally long-legged shore birds with long bills. Some, like the godwits, have upturned bills. Others, like the curlews, have down-curved bills, but most are equipped with straight, sharply pointed bills. Although bill shape and length helps identify members of this large family, field identification is not easy. Almost all have drab winter plumage, generally light below and dark above.

Sizes range from the Least Sandpiper *(Calidris minutilla)* 5 to 6 inches (12.7 to 15.2 cm) long to the Longbilled Curlew *(Numenius americanus)* 26 inches (66 cm) long.

The Eskimo Curlew *(Numenius borealis)* was once the most northern nesting member of the Sandpiper family, but unrestricted hunting late in the 19th century virtually destroyed the species. The last two Eskimo Curlews reported were seen on Martha's Vineyard, Massachusetts, in 1972.

The Willet, 14 to 16¼ inches (35.6 to 41.3 cm) long, including its 2½-inch (6.4 cm) bill, is white below and gray above with black and white wings and a white tail. Its legs and bill are dark blue to black.

It flies with forceful beats of its pointed wings, taking a direct line toward its destination. Often on descent, it locks its wings to glide gracefully to a landing on rocks or sandy beach. Although usually seen wading or walking on the shore, Willets can swim and it is believed that they light on water to rest when migrating over the sea.

Northern limit of the nesting area extends from eastern Oregon northward into the central plains of Canada across

Left: The Willet is a very vocal bird, and its calls—*kreer-reer-reerr* or *pee-wee-wee*—are distinctive. It is particularly noisy when disturbed.

to Nova Scotia. Southern limits, less clearly defined, include Florida and the Gulf Coast of Texas and Mexico, and California. Some birds winter along the north coasts of South America, but most remain in Mexico and the southern United States.

Like many other Sandpipers, Willets were heavily hunted during the 19th century, but protective laws have helped them make a good recovery. Recently, birds have been seen nesting in New England for the first time in more than 100 years.

Willets eat insects, worms, small crabs and fishes, mollusks and some vegetable matter such as seeds and grass shoots. Most food is obtained by probing sand or mud with the sharp bill.

The nest, usually built in loose colonies with other pairs and often on an off-shore island, is a hollow in the sand lined with grass. Four olive-colored eggs spotted with brown are laid from April to May. Incubation, probably done by the female only, takes 22 days. Chicks can leave the nest soon after hatching and begin hunting food for themselves. It is known how old young birds are when they first fly.

Also known as Pied-winged Curlew, Bill-willie and White-winged Curlew, the Willet can fly at a good pace. It has been clocked at 45 miles (72.5 km) an hour.

Above: The American Avocet (*Recurvirostra americana*), a long-legged and long-billed shore bird, breeds in the open marshes and feeds on small crustaceans.
Right: The Marbled Godwit (*Limosa fedoa*) makes loud mating calls during the aerial courtship displays.

The Long-billed Curlew prefers opens spaces, where it feels safest. Except when it is breeding, this bird is very social by nature.

INDEX

BIRDS OF NORTH AMERICA
Picture credits

Jim Anderson, NPS: 84 (left)
Tupper Ansel Blake: 15. 38-39. 66-67. 102-103. 108-109
California Academy of Sciences: 19. 50 (both)
Dick Frear, NPS: 112. 113. 126-127 (both). 130-131. 132-133. 135 (top). 140
C. G. Gebler, NPS: 49
Luther Goldman, USFWS: 65. 81
M. Gregory, California Academy of Sciences: 94
Lloyd G. Ingles, California Academy of Sciences: 2-3. 14 (bottom). 34-35 (both). 36-37. 42-43. 44. 73. 80. 82-83. 86. 88-89. 90-91. 92-93. 95. 96. 99
William S. Keller, NPS: 23 (right). 27 (top)
Carol Lively, USFWS: 61
Wayne Lynch, Parks Canada: 7. 9 (top). 11 (top). 28-29. 30-31. 32. 57. 62-63. 84-85. 100-101. 128 (top). 138-139. 148-149. 150-151. 152. 154-155. 156-157 (both). 158-159. Back Cover
Tom Myers: 14 (top). 58. 64. 104-105. 106. 141
Danny On, Glacier Natural History Association: 1. 24. 107. 142-143

Lloyd Parratt, NPS: 25 (top)
Gordon H. Philp: 54
G.W. Robinson, California Academy of Sciences: 55. 56. 77
Dr. Edward S. Ross: 70-71
Edwin L. Rothfuss: 26
Fred Sibley, USFWS: 45
Glen Smart, USFWS: 144 (bottom)
Gleen Steiner: 114-115. 116-117
Cecil Stoughton, NPS: 129 (top). 144 (top left)
Strauss Collection, California Academy of Sciences: 41
U.S. Fish & Wildlife Service: 16
U.S. National Park Service: 11 (bottom). 12-13. 17. 18 (both). 20-21. 22-23. 25 (bottom). 27 (bottom). 46. 47 (bottom). 48. 59. 69. 72. 76. 79. 87. 109 (right). 122 (top). 128 (bottom). 133 (right). 134 (both). 135 (bottom). 136 (both). 144 (top right)
Utah Department of Wildlife Resource: 33. 98. 129 (bottom). 135 (middle). 153
M.W. Williams, NPS: 10
Bill Yenne: 4-5. 8. 47 (top). 51. 52 (both). 53. 60. 74-75. 78. 92 (left). 97 (both). 110-111. 118 (both). 119. 120. 121. 122. 123. 124-125. 137. 145. 146-147